OUR
FAMILY
FAVOURITES

Si King & Dave Myers

THE HAIRY BIKERS

OUR
FAMILY
FAVOURITES

66 *Writing the series of thirty cookbooks we've produced together has been one of the most fulfilling experiences of my life and of Dave's. Dave and I had started working on this book before he passed away and we were so excited about publishing a new collection of our ideas and recipes – our family favourites. It's something that's very dear to our hearts, as it's about the food we grew up eating, the food we cook for our own families – and that they now cook for themselves. With the very kind support of our publishers and the Hairy Bikers' team, Dave's family and I felt it was right to finish this book in his honour.* 99

Dave and I came together over our love of food. We were already keen cooks when we met, but having been lucky enough to travel five times around the world and having had the chance to savour some of the most wonderful culinary experiences that our beautiful planet has to offer, we became so much more knowledgeable and experienced in the kitchen. And the most important thing for us was to share the knowledge that we gained through our books. With you, our readers, we've cooked together and eaten together as a true community should.

The recipes in this book are ones that both Dave and I love and some – like the sausage balls and the carlin peas – are things we've been cooking for years. There are satisfying brunches, plenty of tasty snacks for those hungry moments and a delicious range of soups and salads. We've included easy family suppers for busy weeknights, plus some fabulous dishes to enjoy preparing at the weekend. And, as always, some sweet treats, ranging from simple pecan fudge to a show-stopping baked Alaska. These are dishes that come from the heart and soul of the Hairy Bikers and our families. They're fun, comforting and always tasty – and some are a bit rock and roll.

Our Family Favourites is an opportunity for me, on behalf of Dave, to say a huge and sincere thank you to you all for the years of support, kindness and joy that we've shared on our journey together.

It's also a way of honouring the love and affection that was shown on 8th June, 2024 – Dave Day. It's not often that I'm left speechless but on that occasion I was. It was overwhelmingly emotional and I still can't put my feelings into words. To receive that amount of love and affection and kindness, to feel that sense of community and fellowship is a rare thing in this modern world. Some 46,000 bikers turned up for the ride and more than 150,000 people waved us on along the way from the Ace Cafe on the North Circular to Dave's hometown of Barrow-in-Furness. On every footbridge, from the very first to the very last, there was someone there for us.

So, thank you all – for the waves, for the smiles, for the banners, for the love you all brought. Dave Day was a true celebration of Dave's life and you would have made him enormously humbled but proud. And I know he would be very proud indeed of this book.

Si xxx

A few top tips

Weigh all your ingredients and use proper measuring spoons and jugs. This is particularly important with baking recipes.

Every oven is different, so be prepared to cook dishes for a shorter or longer time, if necessary. We find a meat thermometer is a useful bit of kit to help you get perfectly cooked meat and chicken. They are readily available online and in kitchen shops.

Peel onions, garlic and other vegetables and fruit unless otherwise specified.

Use free-range eggs whenever possible. We reckon that 95 per cent of good cooking is good shopping – great ingredients need less fussing with – so buy the best and freshest that your budget allows.

We've included a few stock recipes in the last chapter of this book. Stock isn't difficult to make and some home-made stock is great to have in your freezer. But if you don't have time, you can find some good fresh stocks in supermarkets or you can use those little stock pots or cubes.

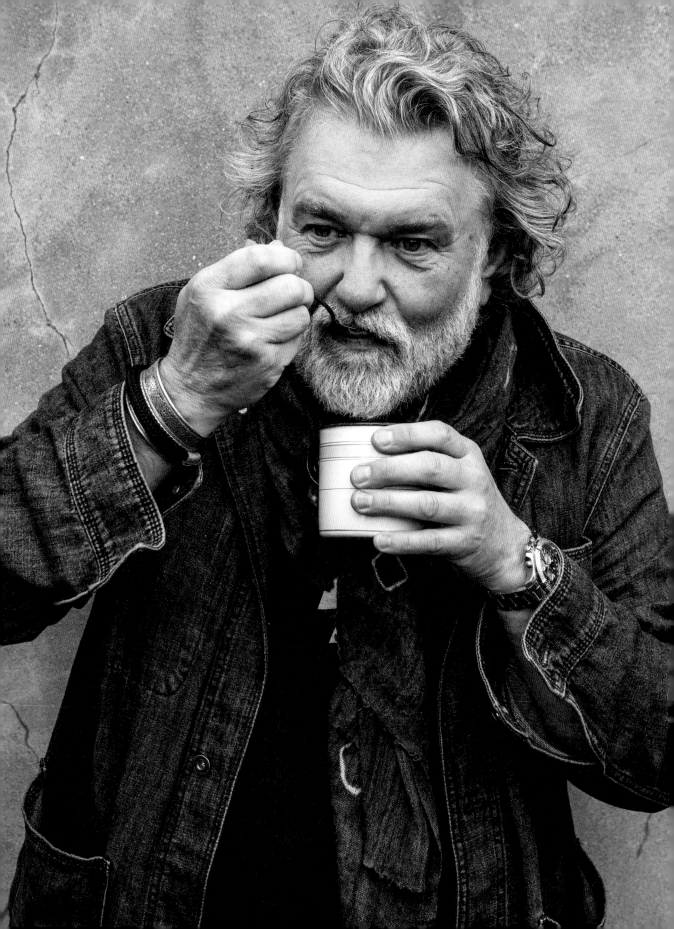

best
brunches

66 I have to admit that it's inevitable when you go five times around the world with your best mate that there are late nights and you get involved with the drinking culture of the countries you visit. As I'm sure you know, Dave and I have always had a penchant for a bit of a knees-up, so we're keen on good brunch recipes for dealing with a hangover – or just feeling a bit rough after the night before. Things like the Argentinian scrambled eggs on page 22 which we ate huge quantities of when we were filming in Buenos Aires, one of our very favourite cities.99

Eggs in holes

4 slices of sourdough
    (or any robust bread)
2 tbsp olive oil
15g butter
4 eggs
2 tbsp finely chopped parsley
pinch of cayenne
a grating of nutmeg
75g Gruyère or any hard
    cheese, grated
salt and black pepper

This is a great favourite with all the King family, especially my eldest son, Alex. It's really an extra-special version of eggy bread, with a bit of spice and some grated cheese thrown in. What's not to love?

1. Take the slices of sourdough and, using a 6–7cm cookie cutter, cut rounds in the middle of each of them. Discard the round centres (they're good for croutons or breadcrumbs or cut them in half and use as half-moon soldiers for boiled eggs).

2. Heat a large frying pan and add a tablespoon of the olive oil. When it's hot, add the slices of bread and fry them on one side only.

3. Remove the bread, then add the remaining olive oil and the butter. When the butter has foamed up, put the bread back in the pan, fried side up. Note – depending on the size of the slices of bread and your pan, you may have to cook these in a couple of batches.

4. Break the eggs one at a time into a ramekin and carefully drop one into each hole. Season with a little salt and pepper. Sprinkle with half the parsley and some cayenne and nutmeg, then add the cheese.

5. Put a cloche over the pan (a large saucepan lid works well) and cook over a low-medium heat for 2–3 minutes until the egg whites are set and the cheese has melted. At this point you can flip the slices over for 30 seconds to brown the cheese a little and give you a few crisp bits around the edges, or you can serve as is. Either way, garnish with the remaining parsley and a little more nutmeg and cayenne if you like.

Savoury bread pudding

SERVES 4

4 eggs
200ml milk
2 tbsp Dijon or wholegrain mustard
300g stale bread, diced
2 tbsp olive oil
1 onion, thinly sliced
½ tsp sugar
150g sauerkraut, well drained and excess liquid squeezed out
1 large dill pickle, finely diced
½ tsp caraway seeds (optional)
butter, for greasing
100g pastrami, torn into strips
100g Gruyère cheese or similar, grated
salt and black pepper

Although this might not win a contest for the most elegant of brunch dishes, just wait till you taste it. Full of great savoury flavours, this has a Reuben sandwich vibe and I believe the world needs more of these pastrami, cheese and pickle combos. For the bread, a light rye sourdough with caraway works well – or a decent bagel.

1. Put the eggs into a large bowl and beat until they're well broken up. Whisk in the milk and season with salt and pepper. Stir in a tablespoon of the mustard, then add the pieces of bread and push them well into the egg and milk mixture. Leave to stand while you get on with the onion.

2. Heat the oil in a frying pan and add the onion. Cook until just translucent, then turn up the heat, sprinkle in the sugar and cook for a few minutes until the slices start to caramelise – the texture should still be quite firm. Remove the pan from the heat and add the sauerkraut, pickle and caraway seeds, if using.

3. Preheat the oven to 200°C/Fan 180°C/Gas 6. Generously butter a shallow ovenproof dish.

4. Add the pastrami to the bread mixture and pile it into the oven dish. Push heaped teaspoons of the onion and sauerkraut, plus the remaining mustard, into the pudding so you get concentrated bursts of flavour throughout. Sprinkle with the cheese.

5. Bake in the preheated oven for 20–25 minutes until the pudding has set and the cheese has melted and browned.

Argentinian scrambled eggs

SERVES 4

1 tbsp olive oil
1 onion, finely chopped
½ red pepper, finely chopped
½ tsp oregano
100g Serrano ham, pulled
    into strips
15g butter
8 eggs, well beaten
small bunch of coriander,
    finely chopped, plus a few
    sprigs reserved for garnish
75g mature Cheddar, grated
500g oven French fries,
    cooked according to
    packet instructions
salt

TO SERVE
hot sauce

A really special version of egg and chips! Every time I cook this dish, it brings back memories of the happy times Dave and I spent together in Argentina. It's nothing short of lush.

1. Heat the olive oil in a large frying pan and add the onion and red pepper. Sauté until the onion is translucent, then add the oregano and ham. Cook for another 30 seconds, then remove the pan from the heat and transfer everything to a plate. Set aside.

2. Wipe out the frying pan and melt the butter. When it's foaming, add the eggs and season them with plenty of salt. Stir over a medium-high heat until the eggs are well scrambled. Add the onion mixture, finely chopped coriander and the cheese to the pan.

3. Roughly chop the fries and add these to the eggs too. Toss everything together, then serve garnished with the reserved coriander sprigs and with hot sauce on the side.

Bloody Maria

2 limes, halved

about 2 tbsp Tajín or similar
Mexican seasoning

4 measures of vodka, tequila
or mezcal (or doubles, of
course)

600ml tomato juice

4 generous dashes of chipotle,
Tabasco or similar Mexican
hot sauce, plus extra if
needed

2 tsp freshly grated
horseradish (optional)

1 tbsp pickled jalapeño juice,
from the jar (optional)

celery salt

TO GARNISH (ALL OPTIONAL)

4 rashers of smoked streaky
bacon

4 celery sticks (preferably
from the centre of the
celery with leaves)

4 pickled jalapeños

4 mint sprigs

Whenever we were on a flight home after a long filming trip, Dave and I always treated ourselves to a Bloody Mary. Our special version of this classic – Mary meets a margarita – has the addition of Mexican Tajín seasoning and it is sensational. Tajín is a mix of lime, chilli peppers and salt and is available online. I'm a big fan of jalapeños and it's great to discover that these chilli peppers are good for you as well as tasty – they're full of vitamins and antioxidants.

1. First make the bacon garnish, if using. Heat a frying pan and add the bacon. Flatten the bacon rashers with something heavy – a steak press works well if you have one or use another heavy-based frying pan or saucepan. Cook until the underside is well browned and lots of fat has rendered out, then flip the rashers over and brown the other side, again weighing them down.

2. Remove from the heat and leave the weight in place as the bacon cools. You will end up with 4 flat, crisp rashers of bacon to use as stirrers.

3. Take 4 tall glasses. Rub lime halves around the rim of each one, then juice the limes. Put the Tajín or Mexican seasoning into a shallow bowl and dip each glass into it so the rims are thickly coated.

4. Add ice to each glass and your choice of spirit. Mix the tomato juice, lime juice and hot sauce together, plus the horseradish and jalapeño pickling juice, if using, then pour into the glasses. Give the drinks a quick stir and add a dash more of the hot sauce if you like. Sprinkle over a generous amount of the Tajín seasoning, followed by some celery salt.

5. Garnish with your choice of bacon and/or celery, jalapeños and mint, then enjoy.

Boxty with spicy eggs

SERVES 4

250g floury potatoes (see method)

1 small onion, very finely chopped

4 tbsp finely chopped coriander (optional)

250g mashed potatoes, chilled

250g plain flour

1 tsp bicarbonate of soda

250–300ml buttermilk

butter, for frying

salt

SPICY EGGS

butter, for frying

4–8 eggs, depending on appetite

2 tsp chipotle paste or similar hot sauce

1 tbsp olive oil

1 tsp red wine or sherry vinegar

juice of ½ lime

4 tomatoes, diced

2 spring onions, finely sliced, to garnish

a few coriander sprigs, finely chopped, to garnish

Boxty are traditional Irish potato pancakes, and with the spicy eggs and the Bloody Maria on the previous page they make the ultimate hair of the dog brunch! If you have the Tajín from making the Bloody Marias on page 24, you could sprinkle a little on these eggs too. The boxty are best served hot from the pan, but they can be made in advance and either kept warm or reheated in a low oven.

1. Coarsely grate the floury potatoes into a tea towel. Bring the tea towel up around the potatoes into a bundle and squeeze well over a bowl to get rid of the excess water. Leave the water to separate – the starch will collect in the bottom of the bowl. Carefully drain off the water, leaving the white starch behind in the bowl – this helps the texture of the boxty. Tip the grated potatoes into the bowl.

2. Add the onion, the coriander, if using, and the mashed potatoes to the bowl. Mix thoroughly. Whisk the flour with the bicarbonate of soda and half a teaspoon of salt. Add this to the bowl and mix again. Finally stir in 250ml of the buttermilk. Combine into a batter, keeping the mixing to an absolute minimum (if you overmix, the end result may be unpleasantly gluey). If the batter is very sticky, add just enough of the remaining buttermilk to loosen it up a bit. Leave to stand for half an hour.

3. Melt a generous amount of butter in a frying pan. Spread half the boxty mixture into the pan and mark a deep cross in it. Fry for 3–4 minutes over a medium heat, until the underside is well browned, then carefully flip the boxty over. Add a little more butter and fry the other side. Turn out on to kitchen paper and repeat with the remaining mixture.

4. For the eggs, heat a generous knob of butter in a large frying pan. When it foams, swirl it around and add the eggs. Season with salt, then fry until cooked to everyone's liking.

5. Mix the chipotle paste or hot sauce with the olive oil, vinegar and lime juice. Add the tomatoes and toss gently together.

6. Serve the warm boxty with the eggs, then spoon the spiced tomatoes over the eggs. Garnish with spring onions and more coriander.

Thai son-in-law eggs

SERVES 4

SHALLOTS

100ml neutral-tasting oil,
    such as groundnut
4½ large shallots, finely sliced

SAUCE

½ shallot, very finely chopped
2 tbsp tamarind purée
2 tbsp fish sauce
35g palm sugar or light brown
    soft sugar
4 lime leaves, roughly bruised
    or pared zest from ½ lime
salt

EGGS

8 eggs, at room temperature
1 tsp curry powder

TO SERVE

2 chillies, finely sliced
leaves from a few coriander
    sprigs
steamed jasmine rice
    (optional)
lime wedges
chilli oil

If you love eggs and spice and you love Thai food, this is the dish for you. It's a traditional favourite in Thailand, featuring eggs that are hard-boiled, then fried and served with a spicy sauce and jasmine rice. There are various stories about the naming of this dish, including mentions of a mother's warning to her son-in-law, but whatever its origins, the flavours make your toes curl with delight.

1. First fry the shallots. Gently heat the oil in a frying pan. When it's warm, not hot, add the shallots, then increase the heat to medium. Cook the shallots until they are crisp and brown, then remove them with a slotted spoon and drain on kitchen paper. Set the pan of oil aside for later.

2. Put all the sauce ingredients into a small saucepan with 2 tablespoons of water. Heat, stirring until the sugar has dissolved and the mixture is the texture of runny honey or maple syrup. Taste and add a little salt if necessary, then remove from the heat and leave to cool. Fish out the lime leaves or zest before serving.

3. Bring a large pan of water to the boil. Carefully lower in the eggs and cook for 7 minutes – this will give you slightly fudgy-textured yolks Remove and cool the eggs in cold water, then peel them and set aside.

4. Reheat the oil the shallots were fried in and add the curry powder. Add the hard-boiled eggs and fry, turning them regularly, until the skins are crisp and probably starting to blister. Remove the eggs from the oil with a slotted spoon and blot on kitchen paper.

5. To assemble, cut the eggs in half and arrange them on a serving dish or on plates. Drizzle over some of the sauce, then top with the chillies, coriander and fried shallots.

6. Serve with rice, if using, as well as more of the sauce, the lime wedges and some chilli oil for extra heat.

Smoked fish & eggs

SERVES 4

2 tbsp olive oil
1 red onion, thinly sliced
2 red peppers, thinly sliced
½ tsp caraway seeds
½ tsp fennel seeds
½ tsp chilli flakes
1 garlic clove, finely chopped
200g cherry tomatoes, puréed
450g baby leaf spinach
250g smoked cod or haddock
    fillet, skinned and cut into
    chunks
a grating of nutmeg
4–8 eggs, depending on
    appetite
4 tbsp crème fraiche
75g Cheddar or Gruyère
    cheese, grated
leaves from a small bunch of
    parsley, finely chopped
salt and black pepper

TO SERVE
buttered toast

We've always loved the combination of smoked fish and eggs in a kedgeree. but in this dish everything is cooked in one pan with lots of veg like a shakshuka, so the eggs absorb all the flavours. A great quick meal for brunch or any time of day. Allow one or two eggs per person depending on appetite.

1. Heat the olive oil in a large sauté pan. Add the red onion and peppers and fry until they're starting to soften. Stir in the caraway and fennel seeds, chilli flakes and garlic and cook for a minute, then add the cherry tomatoes and season with salt and pepper.

2. Bring to the boil, then turn the heat down and simmer until the tomatoes have reduced – the mixture should be quite dry. Add all the spinach and push it down into the pan until it has wilted. Cook, stirring constantly, until the leaves have collapsed and given up most of their moisture – again, the contents of the pan should look fairly dry.

3. Stir in the fish and add a grating of nutmeg, then top with the eggs. Season the eggs, dollop the crème fraiche over them and sprinkle with grated cheese.

4. Cover the pan with a lid and cook gently for at least 7–8 minutes until the egg whites are set, but the yolks are still quite runny. Sprinkle with parsley and serve with some toast.

Eggs with merguez sausages

SERVES 4

1 tbsp olive oil

8 merguez sausages

2 small red onions, cut into slim wedges

200g cherry tomatoes, puréed, or the same amount of passata

½ tsp ground cinnamon (optional)

4–8 hard-boiled eggs (depending on appetite)

leaves from a small bunch of mint

salt and black pepper

COUSCOUS

100g couscous

½ tsp ground cinnamon

½ tsp dried mint

zest of 1 lemon

2 tbsp olive oil

125ml tepid water

TO SERVE

250ml Greek yoghurt

1 tsp dried mint

squeeze of lemon juice

This has to be one of the most comforting brunches or brekkies in the book. With spicy merguez, couscous and the warming flavour of cinnamon, it's a cuddle in a pan.

1. Heat the olive oil in a large frying or sauté pan. Add the merguez sausages and onions and brown them over a high heat. Pour in the tomatoes and season with salt and pepper. Simmer for 5 minutes, then taste and add the cinnamon if the tomatoes need a little extra sweetness.

2. Cut the hard-boiled eggs in half and add them to the pan, sunny-side up. Heat through and garnish with a few mint leaves.

3. Put the couscous in a bowl and mix in the cinnamon, mint and lemon zest. Season with salt and pepper. Drizzle over the olive oil and pour over the tepid water. Cover and leave to stand until all the water is absorbed, then fluff the couscous up with a fork.

4. Mix the yoghurt with the dried mint and season with salt. Serve the sausages and eggs with the couscous, a squeeze of lemon juice and dollops of the yoghurt.

Cowboy baked beans

SERVES 4–6

1 tbsp olive oil
200g smoked bacon, finely
    chopped
1 onion, finely chopped
3 x 400g cans of haricot
    beans, or 750g cooked
    (about 300g dried weight)
1 tsp hot paprika or hot sauce
1 tsp garlic powder
1 tsp dried oregano
400g tomato passata
200ml chicken or ham stock
1 tbsp black treacle
1 tbsp dark soy sauce
1 tbsp light brown soft sugar
2 tsp Worcestershire sauce
15g butter (optional)
black pepper

TO SERVE (OPTIONAL)
fried eggs
sausages

My lovely dad would cook these beans from the back of his Ford Capri in snow, gales, rain or shine, mostly in the sand dunes of Bamburgh beach. I'm including them here as a big thank you to my old pa for introducing me to all these lovely flavours as a young boy. I'm eternally grateful.

1. Heat the olive oil in a large saucepan. Add the bacon and onion and sauté over a high heat until the bacon is crisp and has rendered out plenty of fat and the onion is starting to brown around the edges. Turn down the heat and continue to cook until the onion looks translucent.

2. Stir in the haricot beans, hot paprika or hot sauce, the garlic powder and oregano. Pour over the passata and add the stock. Stir in the treacle, soy sauce, sugar and Worcestershire sauce. Season with black pepper – no need for salt as there's plenty in the bacon, stock and soy sauce.

3. Bring to the boil, then turn the heat down and simmer until the sauce is reduced and thickened. Taste and adjust the flavour as necessary. Stir in the butter, if using, and simmer for a couple more minutes. Serve with fried eggs and/or sausages.

finger food & things on toast

66 One of the most memorable meals that Dave and I ever shared was in Patagonia, during one of our early filming trips. We were in the coastal community of Bahía San Blas and that evening we cleaned some fish we'd just caught, topped it with a chorizo and Parmesan crust and cooked it on the beach by the fishing boats. I'll never forget the look of sheer ecstasy on both our faces as, in the fading light of the Patagonian dusk, we realised that our dreams of combining our love of travel with our love of food and cooking really had come true.99

Parched peas

SERVES 4

500g well-cooked carlin peas
250g vegetable stock or
    cooking liquor from the
    peas (if home-cooked)
1 tbsp cider vinegar
15g butter
salt and black pepper

TO SERVE
salt and malt vinegar

This recipe is a real trip down memory lane. In Cumbria, these pulses are known as pigeon peas, but in Newcastle and the Northeast we call them carlin peas. The tradition is that they're eaten on the fifth Sunday of Lent, known as Carlin Sunday. This isn't actually anything to do with Lent but goes back to a time in the Civil War of 1644, when Royalist Newcastle was under siege from the Scots. People were starving, but relief came in the shape of a cargo of carlin peas which was washed ashore. Carlin peas are still popular all over the north and this recipe is very simple and very delicious.

1. Put the carlin peas in a saucepan with the stock or cooking liquor and the cider vinegar. Season with salt and pepper.

2. Bring to the boil, then turn the heat down to a simmer and cook until most of the liquid has boiled off. You don't want the peas to be completely dry, but they should be looking starchy rather than wet. Stir in the butter.

3. Serve the peas in mugs (enamel mugs are nice), small dishes or paper cones, with plenty of salt and vinegar.

TIP

You can buy cans of carlin peas, but to cook dried carlin peas, first soak them in plenty of water with a teaspoon of salt overnight. The next day, drain the peas and put them in a pan with plenty of fresh water. Bring to the boil and boil fiercely for about 5 minutes, then add a teaspoon of salt and reduce the heat to a gentle simmer. Cook for 30–40 minutes or until tender.

Curried Welsh rarebit

4 large slices of sourdough
2 tsp lime pickle or mango
　　chutney (optional)
4 tomatoes, quite finely diced
a few coriander leaves

CHEESE SAUCE
15g butter
25g flour
2 tsp curry powder
50ml beer
1 small red onion, very finely
　　chopped
1 garlic clove, finely chopped
2 tbsp finely chopped
　　coriander stems
250g hard cheese, such as
　　Cheddar, grated
1 tsp Worcestershire sauce
1 tsp hot sauce (or to taste)
1 egg, beaten

A flavour sensation. If there's a topping for toast that reflects the wonderful multi-cultural nature of our country it's this one. Long live tolerance and understanding in food. When your belly's rumbling and you fancy a snack that's filling and mega tasty, try this.

1. For the sauce, melt the butter in a pan. Stir in the flour and curry powder, then stir to form a roux. Add the beer and continue to stir until smooth.

2. Add all the remaining ingredients except the egg. Stir over a very gentle heat – do not let the mixture boil – until the cheese has melted into the sauce. Leave to cool to room temperature without letting the sauce set completely, then beat in the egg.

3. Heat a grill. Lightly toast the bread, then spread the slices thinly with the lime pickle or chutney, if using. Sprinkle over the tomatoes, then spoon the cheese sauce over the top.

4. Arrange on a rack, then grill until browned and bubbling, turning the slices around as necessary (most grills have hot spots). Serve with a few coriander leaves.

Bacon sandwich with banana ketchup

SERVES 4

12 rashers of smoked bacon
    (streaky or back, or a
    combination)
8 slices of bread, buttered
3 spring onions, finely sliced
½ iceberg lettuce, shredded
    (optional)

COOKED BANANA KETCHUP
1 tbsp olive oil
1 small onion, finely chopped
5g root ginger, finely chopped
3 garlic cloves, finely chopped
1 scotch bonnet, deseeded
    depending on how hot you
    want the ketchup, chopped
½ tsp Caribbean curry
    powder
½ tsp ground allspice
¼ tsp ground cinnamon
¼ tsp ground nutmeg
1 tsp dried thyme
3 bananas, peeled and roughly
    broken up
1 tbsp light brown soft sugar
juice and zest of 1 lime
2 tsp cider vinegar
salt and black pepper

I discussed this recipe at length with Dave. He spent some time filming in South Africa a while back and he raved about these sandwiches which loomed large in his culinary memories. The cooked version of the amazing banana ketchup is quick to make. but if you're in too much of a hurry. try our special instant ketchup – see the tip below. Either way. this is a great sandwich that also gives a nod to Caribbean flavours.

1. To make the ketchup, heat the olive oil in a small saucepan. Add the onion and cook over a medium-high heat until it is softening and turning dark brown around the edges.

2. Add the ginger, garlic and scotch bonnet. Stir for a minute, then add all the other ingredients and season with salt and pepper. Stir until the sugar has dissolved, mashing the bananas into the other ingredients. Add 100ml of water and cook for another couple of minutes, stirring constantly. Blitz into a paste and store in the fridge in a sterilised jar. This ketchup keeps for a couple of weeks.

3. To make the sandwich, grill the bacon until crisp. Spread one side of each slice of bread liberally with the banana ketchup and sandwich the bacon, spring onions and lettuce, if using, in between.

TIP

If you don't have time to make the cooked ketchup, try this. Simply peel a banana and put it in a food processor with a tablespoon of scotch bonnet sauce, the juice of half a lime and 2 teaspoons of sugar, then blitz. Use this ketchup straight away.

Chopped boiled eggs on toast

SERVES 4

1 small red onion, finely chopped and soaked in salted water for 30 minutes

4 medium tomatoes, finely chopped

50g wafer-thin ham, finely chopped

4–8 eggs, depending on appetite, at room temperature

4 generous knobs of butter

sprinkling of cayenne powder

50g hard cheese, such as Cheddar, grated (optional)

a few parsley sprigs, finely chopped, to garnish

salt and black pepper

TO SERVE

hot buttered toast

In my family, whenever anyone was feeling under the weather, my mam or my sister would prepare these chopped boiled eggs to get us back on our feet. Simple, comforting and delicious. It's always been a much-loved dish in the King household and something we eat to this day. My little granddaughter enjoys it now too.

1. Drain the red onion and mix it with the tomatoes and ham. Season with salt and pepper, then set aside.

2. Prepare a bowl of iced water. Bring a saucepan of water to the boil and lower in the eggs. Boil them for 4½–5 minutes, depending on size, then remove the eggs from the boiling water and plunge them into the bowl of iced water. Peel the eggs once they are cool enough to handle.

3. Put a slice of toast on each plate. Break the eggs over the toast, then roughly chop them – this makes sure all the runny yolk goes over the toast, rather than over your chopping board. Add a generous knob of butter to the eggs and season with salt and pepper. Sprinkle over the cayenne, followed by the cheese, if using.

4. Sprinkle over the onion, tomato and ham mixture, then garnish with the parsley. Serve at once.

Mushrooms (& kidneys) on toast

SERVES 4

SAUCE

1 tbsp olive oil
2 shallots, very finely chopped
4 garlic cloves, finely chopped
1 rosemary sprig
1 thyme sprig
1 bay leaf
½ tsp lightly crushed black
    peppercorns
250ml red wine
250ml well-flavoured beef
    stock
salt

BEURRE MANIÉ (OPTIONAL)

1 tsp butter
1 tsp plain flour

MUSHROOMS & KIDNEYS

6 kidneys, quartered and
    cored (optional)
1–2 tbsp olive oil (depending
    on whether you are
    cooking kidneys)
1 small red onion, very finely
    sliced
400g chestnut mushrooms

TO SERVE

hot buttered toast
a few parsley leaves, finely
    chopped
a few chives, finely snipped

My dad introduced me to the wonders that are kidneys. He loved them and for some reason they always seemed to be available at sea – Dad was in the Navy. The sauce can be made well in advance if you want, and the mushrooms and kidneys can be added at the last minute.

1. Start by making the sauce. Heat the oil in a saucepan, add the shallots and sauté them for a few minutes until they are starting to take on some colour. Add the garlic, herbs and black peppercorns and stir for another minute or so.

2. Pour in the red wine and bring to the boil, then keep at a rolling boil until the wine has reduced by half. Add the beef stock, bring back to the boil and continue to boil until the volume has reduced by half again. The sauce should be thick enough to coat the back of a spoon, but if it isn't, thicken with a beurre manié. To do this, mix the butter and flour together to form a paste. Add it to the sauce, whisking it over a low heat until it has thickened. Strain the sauce before serving.

3. If serving the kidneys, season them with salt. Heat a tablespoon of olive oil in a large frying pan, add the kidneys and sear them for a couple of minutes on both sides. Remove them from the pan and set aside.

4. Heat another tablespoon of oil in the pan and add the red onion. Fry until lightly browned, then add the mushrooms, season with salt and fry briskly until lightly browned. Put the kidneys, if using, back in the pan and toss everything together.

5. Pile the contents of the pan on to hot buttered toast. Pour the sauce into the frying pan, stirring to deglaze the base of the pan, and bring to the boil. Spoon the sauce over the mushrooms and kidneys, if using, and garnish with a little parsley and a few chopped chives.

TIP

If you want to make this even more delicious, add some bone marrow. Heat the bone marrow in a separate small frying pan. Add the fat from the marrow to the sauce, then finely chop the remaining solids very, very finely and add them to the sauce after straining.

Corn ribs with roast tomato salsa

SERVES 4

4 corn on the cobs
4 tbsp olive oil
juice of 1 lime
1 tsp garlic powder
1 tsp dried oregano
1 tsp hot sauce
salt and black pepper

ROAST TOMATO SALSA
250g tomatoes
up to 1 tbsp olive oil (optional)
4 garlic cloves, unpeeled
100g cream cheese
50g soured cream
2 tsp red wine vinegar
zest of ½ lime
1–2 tsp hot sauce or chilli
    powder
½ tsp smoked paprika

GARLIC & LIME BUTTER
50g butter
2 garlic cloves, crushed
leaves from a few parsley
    or coriander sprigs, very
    finely chopped
zest of 1 lime

I love this recipe. It pleases everyone, gets you a bit sticky and messy and it's really good to eat. If you have an air fryer you could cook the ribs in that. They'll take about the same time as in the oven.

1. Preheat the oven to 200°C/Fan 180°C/Gas 6.

2. First prepare the corn. Cut each cob in half widthways, then cut each piece into 4–6 ribs, depending on how fat your cobs are – the ribs should be 3 or 4 kernels wide.

3. Put the olive oil, lime juice, garlic powder, oregano and hot sauce in a large bowl and mix together. Add the corn ribs and season with plenty of salt and pepper. Toss so the ribs are well coated, then spread them over a large baking tray.

4. Roughly chop the tomatoes and put them in the same bowl the corn was in. Toss so they take on the residue of oil left in the bowl. This should be enough but add a little more oil if you like. Season the tomatoes with salt and pepper and tip them into a roasting tin.

5. Put the tomatoes in the oven. After 10 minutes, add the garlic cloves to the tomatoes, then put the tray of corn in the oven too. Roast both the corn ribs and the tomatoes for a further 20–25 minutes, turning the ribs halfway through, until they are nicely charred and the tomatoes are sticky and collapsed.

6. While the vegetables are roasting, prepare the garlic and lime butter. Melt the butter in a saucepan and add the garlic. Cook for another couple of minutes, just to take the sting out of the garlic, then stir in the herbs and lime zest.

7. Put the cream cheese in a bowl and break it up with a fork. Beat in the soured cream, along with the red wine vinegar, lime zest, hot sauce or chilli powder and the smoked paprika.

8. Remove the corn ribs and tomatoes from the oven. Tip the tomatoes into a food processor. Squeeze the garlic flesh out of the skins and add it to the processor, then blitz until quite smooth. Stir this into the cream cheese mixture.

9. Brush the corn ribs liberally with the garlic and lime butter and arrange them on a serving dish. Serve with the roasted tomato dip. You could add a dusting of Tajín if you have some leftover from making the Bloody Marias on page 24.

Roast cauliflower with tahini sauce

SERVES 4

1 large cauliflower
2 tbsp olive oil
1 tsp nigella seeds
1 tsp chilli flakes
zest of 1 lemon
75g Cheddar or Gruyère
    cheese, grated (optional)
1 tbsp za'atar
salt and black pepper

TAHINI SAUCE
4 tbsp tahini
1 garlic clove, crushed
juice of 1 lemon
1 tsp honey

Roast cauliflower, nigella seeds and tahini are a combo made in heaven. I'm a biker, so trust me when I tell you that this is epic. By the way, if you leave out the cheese and use a bit of maple syrup instead of honey, this makes a good vegan dish.

1. Preheat the oven to 200°C/Fan 180°C/Gas 6. Separate the cauliflower into florets, stems and leaves. Roughly chop any of the larger leaves.

2. Put the cauliflower in a large roasting tin and drizzle over the olive oil. Toss well to ensure everything is evenly coated, then sprinkle over the nigella seeds, chilli flakes and lemon zest. Season with salt and pepper and sprinkle over the grated cheese, if using.

3. Roast in the oven for 15–20 minutes, shaking the tin regularly, until the cauliflower is lightly charred in places and the stems are knife tender.

4. While the cauliflower is roasting, make the sauce. Mix the tahini in a bowl with the garlic and lemon juice. You will find that the tahini seizes up and thickens when you stir in the lemon juice. Add the honey and just enough water to give the sauce a thick, pouring consistency.

5. Sprinkle the za'atar over the cauliflower and serve with the tahini sauce on the side.

Halloumi dippers with harissa mayo

SERVES 4

2 x 225g blocks of halloumi
1 tsp dried mint
1 tsp oregano
2 tbsp plain flour
1 egg
100g panko breadcrumbs
2 tbsp olive oil
salt and black pepper

HARISSA MAYO
6 tbsp mayonnaise
2 tbsp harissa
½ tsp dried mint
juice and zest of ½ lemon

Please, please, please make these. I love them. Baking is the easiest way to go, but you could also shallow fry the halloumi dippers or cook them in an air fryer. In an air fryer, cook them for about 15 minutes at 200°C.

1. Preheat the oven to 200°C/Fan 180°C/Gas 6. Line a large baking tray with baking parchment.

2. Cut each block of halloumi into 12 chips. Put the mint, oregano and flour in a shallow bowl and add salt, then mix thoroughly. Beat the egg in another shallow bowl and put the breadcrumbs into a third bowl.

3. Dip the halloumi chips into the flour mixture and pat off the excess. Then dip them into the egg, and lastly, coat thoroughly in the breadcrumbs. Arrange them on the baking tray, then brush with the oil and place in the oven. Bake for about 20 minutes until the halloumi is soft and squidgy and the coating is crisp and golden brown.

4. To make the dip, put the mayonnaise in a bowl with the harissa, mint and lemon juice and zest. Season with salt and pepper and mix thoroughly, then taste and add more lemon juice or harissa if necessary.

5. Serve the halloumi dippers with the harissa mayo.

Spicy crab & cheese dip

SERVES 4

butter, for greasing
150g cream cheese
100g soured cream or crème
    fraiche
2 tsp Dijon mustard
1 tsp garlic powder
½ tsp cayenne powder
1 tsp Worcestershire sauce
50g brown crab meat
75g white crab meat
zest of 1 lime
125g mature Cheddar, grated
4 spring onions, finely
    chopped
2 tbsp pickled jalapeños,
    roughly chopped
a few coriander leaves, finely
    chopped
salt and black pepper

TO SERVE
buttered toast
raw vegetables
lime wedges

Crab meat is a real treat but it is expensive, so if you're looking for a recipe to make it go a long way, search no further. This is rich and delicious and dead simple to make. Enjoy it as a dip with sticks of raw veg or pile it on to buttered toast. If you're serving this as a light meal, a tomato salad on the side is good.

1. Preheat the oven to 180°C/Fan 160°C/Gas 4. Butter a medium-sized ovenproof dish.

2. Put the cream cheese in a bowl and beat until smooth. Add the soured cream or crème fraiche, mustard, garlic powder, cayenne, Worcestershire sauce and brown crab meat. Beat again until smooth and well combined.

3. Fold in the white crab meat, lime zest, 75g of the grated cheese and most of the spring onions – reserve some of the green tops for a garnish. Pile everything into the buttered dish and sprinkle over the remaining cheese and the jalapeños.

4. Bake in the preheated oven for about 25 minutes until the cheese has melted and the dip is piping hot. Sprinkle with the reserved spring onion greens and coriander before serving with buttered toast, raw vegetables and lime wedges.

Pea & feta dip

SERVES 4

200g feta cheese, crumbled
50g Greek yoghurt
200g frozen peas, blanched
    for 1 minute
1 garlic clove, finely chopped
1 tsp dried mint
½ tsp dried oregano
zest and juice of ½ lime
3 spring onions, finely
    chopped
extra virgin olive oil, for
    drizzling
pinch of cayenne powder
pinch of ground allspice
salt and black pepper

TO SERVE
toast or crackers
Serrano ham (optional)

We're not as green as we are pea-looking to paraphrase the old saying! The creaminess of the yoghurt with the salty feta and the earthy note of the peas all work together to make a very tasty dip, with the little nod of spice giving the finishing touch. Great as is, but this is also good piled on to toast or bruschetta. Word of warning – once you start eating this dip it's hard to stop.

1. Set aside 25g of the feta. Put the rest in a food processor and process it until well broken down and as smooth as possible. Add the yoghurt and blitz again.

2. Reserve 2 tablespoons of the peas for a garnish, then add the rest to the food processor, along with the garlic, mint, oregano, lime zest and all but a tablespoon of the spring onions. Season with a little salt and black pepper. Continue to process until you have a fairly smooth dip, then scoop it into a bowl or container and chill for at least half an hour to firm it up a little.

3. Beat in a little of the lime juice. Garnish with the reserved peas, feta and spring onions, then drizzle over the remaining lime juice and a generous amount of olive oil. Sprinkle with more salt, the cayenne and allspice. Serve with toast or crackers and some Serrano ham on the side is nice if you fancy.

Sweetcorn fritters with lime & sriracha dip

SERVES 4

350g sweetcorn (preferably fresh or frozen, not tinned)

1 tbsp olive oil

4 spring onions, finely chopped

1 large chilli, finely chopped

1 tsp smoked paprika

1 tsp garlic powder

2 tbsp finely chopped coriander stems

100g plain flour

50g fine cornmeal

½ tsp baking powder

2 eggs

100ml buttermilk

oil (olive or something neutral like groundnut), for shallow frying

salt and black pepper

LIME & SRIRACHA DIP

100g soured cream

100g yoghurt

2 tbsp sriracha

zest of 1 lime

juice of ½ lime

a few coriander leaves, finely chopped (optional)

Dave and I have developed a number of sweetcorn fritter recipes over the years, but I think this is my favourite. The zingy lime and sriracha dip sets the fritters off a treat. A perfect contrast of flavour and texture.

1. Roughly purée 100g of the sweetcorn and set it aside. Heat the olive oil in a frying pan and add the remaining whole kernels and a pinch of salt. Fry the kernels over a high heat until starting to brown – this will give a nice smoky flavour to the finished fritters. Add the spring onions and cook for another couple of minutes, then stir in the chilli, paprika, garlic powder and coriander stems. Remove from the heat and leave to cool.

2. Whisk the plain flour, cornmeal and baking powder together in a bowl and season with plenty of salt and pepper. Make a well and add the eggs, then, starting from the middle, work them into the flour to make a thick paste. Add the buttermilk and beat until smooth, then fold in the sweetcorn mixture and the puréed sweetcorn.

3. Coat the base of a frying pan with oil. Take heaped tablespoons of the sweetcorn batter and drop them into the oil. Fry the fritters until brown on the underside, then flip them over and continue to cook until they are crisp and well browned. Drain them on kitchen paper. You'll need to cook the fritters in 3 or 4 batches.

4. To make the dip, mix everything together, including the coriander leaves, if using, and season with salt and pepper. Serve the fritters hot, with the dip on the side.

Buttermilk chicken dippers

SERVES 4 OR MORE

3 boneless, skinless
    chicken breasts
150g plain flour
vegetable oil, for frying
salt and black pepper

MARINADE
300ml buttermilk
1 tsp garlic powder
1 tsp mustard powder
1 tsp dried thyme

MUSTARD MAYONNAISE
200g mayonnaise
2 tbsp Dijon mustard
1 tsp dried thyme
dash of Worcestershire sauce
squeeze of lemon juice
dash of hot sauce (optional)

I've cooked these for years, first for my own boys and now for my grandchildren. I like to introduce kids to loads of different flavours, including herbs and spices, so they grow up appreciating good food. My granddaughter Ada loves these and while little George only has four teeth, you can tell he's enjoying his food by his smiles and the grunting sounds he makes as he eats.

1. Take each chicken breast and remove the mini fillet that's usually attached to the back. Slice each breast in half horizontally. To do this, put a breast on your work surface, place your hand on top and slice in from the side to give you 2 pieces of an even thickness. Then slice each piece and the mini fillets into slim goujons, across the grain.

2. Mix the marinade ingredients together with a teaspoon of salt and lots of black pepper. Add the chicken pieces and stir well to coat them all, then leave to marinate in the fridge for several hours or overnight.

3. Remove the chicken from the fridge half an hour before you want to cook it. Preheat the oven to 160°C/Fan 140°C/Gas 3.

4. Put the plain flour into a shallow bowl or plate and season with salt. Remove the chicken pieces from the marinade and dip them into the flour, coating each one well before shaking off the excess.

5. Coat the base of a large frying pan with oil and place it over a medium-high heat. When the oil is hot, add some of the chicken pieces – don't overcrowd the pan or the chicken will steam, not fry, and won't crisp up nicely. Cook the chicken pieces on each side for 2–3 minutes until crisp and golden brown. Drain on kitchen paper, then transfer to a baking tray and keep warm in the oven while you cook the next batch.

6. To make the mustard mayonnaise, mix all the ingredients together and season with salt and pepper. Taste and add more Worcestershire sauce, lemon juice or hot sauce to get the flavour you like.

7. Serve the chicken dippers with the mustard mayonnaise.

Glazed chicken wings

SERVES 4

12 chicken wings
salt

MARINADE
2 tbsp dark soy sauce
1 tbsp sriracha
1 tsp garlic powder
1 tsp honey
1 tbsp apricot jam
juice of ½ lime
1 tsp sesame oil

TO SERVE
2 spring onions, finely
    chopped
soured cream, mixed with
    some crumbled blue cheese
    (optional)

I have a reputation for being able to strip the meat off a chicken wing in one go and part of the reason for this is simply because I love them. Serve these wings whole with just the tips removed (save them for stock) or split the wings in half.

1. Mix all the marinade ingredients together and add salt. Add the chicken wings and stir to make sure they are all properly coated. Leave them to marinate for at least half an hour – if you want to leave them for longer, transfer them to the fridge.

2. Preheat the oven to 180°C/Fan 160°C/Gas 4. Line a baking tray with baking parchment.

3. Remove the wings from the marinade, scraping off any excess, and place them on the tray. Bake in the oven for about 40 minutes, turning twice during that time and basting with any remaining marinade.

4. Remove from the oven and sprinkle over the spring onions.

Sausage balls with Worcestershire sauce

SERVES 4

1 tbsp olive oil

8 large sausages, skinned

200ml Worcestershire sauce

2 tsp sesame oil

1 tbsp sesame seeds

Simple is so often best and you can't get much more simple than this recipe. These sausage balls are nothing short of fabulous and a winner at parties – the King family rarely have a gathering without them. Give them a try and I'm sure you'll agree.

1. Heat the olive oil in a large frying pan. Divide each sausage into 3 and roll the pieces into balls.

2. Add the sausage balls to the pan and brown them on at least 2 sides, then pour the Worcestershire sauce into the pan around them. Bring to the boil and simmer until the Worcestershire sauce has reduced to a sticky syrup around the sausages. Keep turning the sausage balls over in the sauce as it reduces.

3. Drizzle over the sesame oil and sprinkle over the sesame seeds – they should stick well. Leave the sausage balls for a few minutes if you can bear to before eating, as they will be very hot!

soups & salads

66 Friendship is a wonderful thing and like most people, I've always said I'm willing to do anything for my best mate. This was put to the test one time after Dave had a motorcycle accident and broke his arm and wrist. He had a cast on his arm and couldn't do much for himself, including washing properly. So, there I am with him standing stark naked in the shower and he says: 'Kingy, would you mind awfully washing my armpits?' I agreed – he was a clean man – but then he started singing 'Je t'aime'. I looked him in the eye and said: 'If there's any movement down below, I'm off.' 99

Colcannon soup

SERVES 4

25g butter
1 onion, diced
1 leek, diced
500g floury potatoes, diced
    (peeling optional)
3 garlic cloves, finely chopped
½ pointed cabbage or 200g
    kale, shredded
1 large thyme sprig
1 bay leaf
800ml vegetable or chicken
    stock
100ml single cream
a few chives, finely snipped,
    to serve
salt and black pepper

GARNISH (OPTIONAL)
1 tbsp olive oil
100g black or white pudding
    or sausage meat, crumbled
1 tsp mustard powder or
    mustard
2 tsp cider or sherry vinegar
dash of Tabasco or similar hot
    sauce
dash of Worcestershire sauce

A firm favourite for the cooler months, this hearty soup is full of comfort and when you add the garnish, it becomes a proper filling main course. Great for Bonfire Night, which is when our families normally eat this. I think chicken stock is best here, but obviously use veggie if you prefer.

1. Heat the butter in a large saucepan. Add the onion, leek and potatoes. Stir to coat the vegetables with the melted butter, then sauté for several minutes until the onion is looking translucent. Add the garlic and the cabbage or kale. Stir until the leaves have collapsed down a little, then add the thyme, bay leaf and stock. Season with salt and pepper.

2. Bring the soup to the boil, then turn the heat down and simmer, partially covered, for 10-15 minutes until the vegetables are tender.

3. Remove the thyme and bay leaf, then pour in the cream and simmer for a further minute. Give the soup a quick whizz with a stick blender or put half the soup in a jug blender for a brief burst before pouring it back in the saucepan. The idea is to break it down enough to thicken but still keep plenty of texture. You can, of course, blend the soup until smooth if that's what you prefer. Check the seasoning and add more salt and black pepper to taste.

4. If you're making the garnish, heat the oil. Add the black or white pudding or sausage meat and fry until well browned and cooked through. Add the mustard powder or mustard, the vinegar, hot sauce and Worcestershire sauce and cook for another 2–3 minutes.

5. Serve the soup piping hot, sprinkled with the snipped chives and the garnish, if using.

Pinto bean & coconut stew

SERVES 4

1 tbsp olive or coconut oil
2 small red onions, cut into
    slim wedges
1 red pepper, diced
1 green pepper, diced
1 tsp cumin seeds
3 garlic cloves, finely chopped
250g squash or pumpkin,
    peeled and diced
2 courgettes, diced
½ tsp ground cinnamon
½ tsp ground allspice
1 tsp dried oregano
2 bay leaves
2 x 400g cans of pinto beans,
    drained (or 200g dried
    beans, cooked)
2 x 400g cans of coconut milk
zest and juice of ½ lime
2 tbsp sherry
salt and black pepper

TOMATO SALSA
1 small red onion, finely
    chopped
100g tomatoes, finely
    chopped
1 jalapeño chilli or similar,
    finely chopped
2 tsp red wine or sherry
    vinegar
zest and juice of ½ lime
pinch of ground cinnamon
1 tbsp olive oil
a few coriander leaves or a few
    fresh oregano leaves, finely
    chopped

Pulses, spice and coconut milk make a wonderfully mellow and creamy stew that's topped with chilli and lime salsa to add a bit of zest and heat. It's enough to make any vegan in your family very happy indeed. Mega delicious.

1. For the salsa, put everything in a bowl and season with salt and pepper. Leave to stand for at least half an hour.

2. Heat the olive or coconut oil in a heavy-based saucepan or a flameproof casserole dish Add the red onions and peppers and fry them over a medium heat until the onion is taking on some colour. Add the cumin seeds, garlic, squash or pumpkin and courgettes and cook for a further minute, then stir in the spices and herbs.

3. Add the pinto beans and coconut milk to the pan. Season with salt and pepper, then bring to the boil. Turn down the heat and simmer, partially covered, until the sauce has thickened and the vegetables are tender.

4. To finish the stew, add the lime zest and juice and half the sherry. Taste and add more seasoning and sherry to your liking. Serve with spoonfuls of the tomato salsa.

TIP

If you want to cook a batch of dried beans (cheaper than using cans), here's a guide to quantities. You can freeze any you don't use immediately. You'll find that 250g of dried beans gives you 600g cooked; 500g of dried beans gives you 1.2kg cooked.

Our ribollita

SERVES 4

2 tbsp olive oil
1 onion, finely chopped
2 carrots, finely sliced
2 celery sticks, finely sliced
200g cavolo nero or swiss
   chard, stems and leaves
   separated
4 garlic cloves, finely chopped
100ml red or white wine
   (optional)
1 bouquet garni made up of
   2 bay leaves, 1 thyme sprig,
   1 parsley sprig, 1 rosemary
   sprig
1 strip of pared lemon zest
500ml chicken or vegetable
   stock or water
400g can of chopped
   tomatoes
2 x 400g cans of cannellini
   beans, drained, or 500g
   cooked beans
200g butternut squash,
   peeled and diced
1 leek, sliced
1 Parmesan rind (optional)
1 courgette, diced
salt and black pepper

GARLIC CROUTONS
200g stale bread (ciabatta,
   Tuscan bread, or any good
   sourdough)
2 tbsp olive oil
1 garlic clove, sliced
2 tbsp finely chopped parsley

TO SERVE
a few basil leaves
chilli flakes
good extra virgin olive oil

Dave and I have always loved this classic bean soup from Tuscany. It's just epic. I maintain to this day that the best ribollita I've ever eaten was made by my big sister, who's lived in Italy for nearly thirty years. Traditionally, you simply add stale bread to the soup, but I like to make these croutons for an extra kick of garlic. A popular choice with the Hairy Biker team.

1. Heat the olive oil in a large saucepan and add the onion, carrots and celery. Finely chop the stems of the cavolo nero or chard and add those to the pan too. Season with salt and pepper and cook gently, stirring regularly, for about 15 minutes until the vegetables have started to soften and take on some colour.

2. Add the garlic and stir for a minute, then pour in the wine, if using, and leave it to bubble up and evaporate. Drop in the bouquet garni and the lemon zest, then pour over the stock or water and the chopped tomatoes. Roughly purée half the beans, then add them and the whole beans to the saucepan. Roughly tear the cavolo nero or chard leaves and push these into the soup, along with the squash and leek. Tuck in the Parmesan rind if you have one.

3. Bring the soup to the boil, then turn the heat down to a simmer. Partially cover the pan and leave to simmer for another 15 minutes, then add the courgette. Continue to cook for a further 10 minutes until all the vegetables are tender, then fish out the bouquet garni, lemon zest and the Parmesan rind, if using.

4. For the garlic croutons, tear the stale bread into rough pieces. Heat the olive oil in a large frying pan and add the garlic. As soon as it starts to take on some colour, remove it with a slotted spoon. Add the bread and season with plenty of salt, then stir the bread into the olive oil until it is crisp and browned. Stir in the parsley.

5. To serve, divide the bread between your bowls, then ladle over the soup. Garnish with basil leaves, chilli flakes and a drizzle of extra virgin olive oil.

Chicken & bacon ramen

SERVES 4

2 tbsp dark soy sauce

2 tbsp light soy sauce

1 tbsp mirin

1 tsp honey

1 tsp gochujang

2 garlic cloves, crushed

2 or 3 boneless, skinless
   chicken breasts
   (depending on size)

BROTH

6 rashers of smoked bacon
   (streaky or back or a
   combination), halved

1.5 litres chicken or chicken
   and pork stock (see p.271)

6 garlic cloves, finely sliced

15g root ginger, sliced into
   fine matchsticks

1 red pepper, cut into strips

200g long-stemmed broccoli

TO FINISH

200g dried ramen noodles,
   cooked according to packet
   instructions

1 piece of nori, cut into strips

4 spring onions, sliced on the
   diagonal

a few drops of sesame oil

chilli oil or hot sauce, to serve

When you fancy a ramen, nothing else will do and this is a really gutsy version with chicken and bacon – woo hoo! You can, of course, make the soup with a good chicken stock, but if you want to go the extra mile, try using our special chicken and pork stock with the addition of a pig's trotter for extra flavour. You'll find the recipe on page 271. Gochujang is a chilli paste, popular in Korean cooking and available in supermarkets.

1. Put the soy sauces, mirin, honey and gochujang into a bowl with the garlic and stir. Add the chicken breasts and combine, then leave them in the fridge to marinate for several hours or overnight.

2. When you're ready to make the broth, heat a large saucepan, add the bacon and fry until crisp and browned. There's no need to add oil, as the fat will start rendering out almost immediately. Remove the bacon from the saucepan and set aside.

3. Add the stock to the saucepan along with the garlic and ginger and bring to the boil. Remove the chicken from the marinade and add this too, reserving the marinade. Turn down the heat to the barest simmer and cook for 10 minutes. Remove the chicken breasts from the broth, then slice them thinly across the grain. Set aside.

4. Add half the reserved marinade to the broth with the red pepper and broccoli and cook for 4–5 minutes until the veg are just tender. Taste the broth and add the rest of the marinade if you think it necessary.

5. To finish, divide the noodles, nori, bacon and chicken between your bowls. Use tongs to remove the pieces of broccoli and red pepper from the broth and add these to the bowls too. Ladle over the broth and garnish with the spring onions, then add a few drops of sesame oil.

6. Serve with chilli oil or hot sauce at the table.

Filipino pork menudo

SERVES 4

2 tbsp soy sauce
zest and juice of ½ lime
juice of ½ mandarin or
    clementine
750g pork shoulder, diced
2 tbsp olive oil
1 onion, finely chopped
2 large carrots, cut into slices
    on the diagonal
1 green pepper, finely
    chopped
100g liver (chicken, lamb or
    pig), finely diced
3 frankfurters, sliced on the
    diagonal (optional)
4 garlic cloves, finely chopped
1 tbsp tomato purée
2 bay leaves
400g can of tomatoes
250ml chicken stock
500g potatoes, cut into
    chunks (peeling optional)
25g raisins
2 red peppers, cut into strips
1 tbsp fish sauce
salt and black pepper

TO SERVE (OPTIONAL)
steamed rice
pak choi

If you fancy something a little different but wholesome, warm and tasty, this is for you. Menudo is a stew-like soup that's popular both in Mexico and other Latin American countries, as well as in the Philippines, and our recipe is based on the Filipino version. I just love the variety of flavours and textures in this and although we've made the frankfurters optional, I urge you to include them. They make the dish so satisying. The traditional marinade contains calamansi juice – the calamansi is a citrus fruit native to the Philippines – but it's fine to use a mixture of lime and clementine or mandarin juice instead.

1. First marinate the pork. Put the soy sauce and the citrus zest and juice into a bowl. Add the pork and stir to coat, then leave it to stand while you prepare the other ingredients.

2. Heat the oil in a large saucepan. Add the onion, carrots and green pepper and sauté until soft and translucent, then turn up the heat and allow them to brown slightly.

3. Strain the pork, reserving the marinade liquid. Add the pork, liver and the frankfurters, if using, to the pan. Brown them all over a high heat, then add the garlic and stir for another minute.

4. Stir in the tomato purée, then add the bay leaves and tinned tomatoes. Pour in the chicken stock and stir to make sure nothing is sticking to the bottom of the pan. Season with salt and pepper.

5. Bring to the boil, then cover the pan and turn the heat down to a simmer. Cook for half an hour, then add the potatoes, raisins and red peppers. Pour in the reserved marinade along with the fish sauce. Bring to the boil again, then turn down the heat and simmer, partially covered, for another 25–30 minutes until the potatoes and peppers are tender. Stir regularly, keeping an eye on the level of liquid. Add a splash of water or more stock if necessary.

6. Serve the menudo in shallow bowls or over rice.

Chicken & mushroom soup

SERVES 4

1 tbsp olive oil
15g butter
1 small onion, very finely
    chopped
250g button mushrooms,
    finely sliced
10g dried mushrooms (porcini
    or wild), soaked in 50ml of
    freshly boiled water
1 chicken breast, diced
3 garlic cloves
leaves from 1 thyme sprig
leaves from 2 tarragon sprigs,
    finely chopped
1 dill frond, left whole
zest of 1 lemon
1 heaped tbsp plain flour
4 tbsp Marsala wine or sherry
750ml chicken or mushroom
    stock
100ml single cream or
    buttermilk
salt and black pepper

GARNISH
1 tbsp olive oil
250g portobellini mushrooms
1 garlic clove, finely chopped
pinch of ground allspice
leaves from a few tarragon
    or dill sprigs, very finely
    chopped
a swirl of single cream
    (optional)

Yes, this is a chicken and mushroom soup, but not as you know it. The cream or buttermilk is added here more for taste than thickening and makes for a light and flavoursome soup. A long-established favourite in both the King and Myers households.

1. Heat the oil in a large pan and add the butter. When the butter foams, add the onion and sauté until it's soft and translucent. Turn up the heat slightly, add the button mushrooms and fry them until lightly browned.

2. Strain the dried mushrooms, reserving the soaking liquor, and finely chop them. Add them to the saucepan along with the diced chicken breast. Fry until the chicken is lightly browned, then stir in the garlic, herbs and lemon zest. Cook for another minute, then stir in the flour and cook for a couple of minutes.

3. Pour in 3 tablespoons of the Marsala or sherry, followed by the stock and season with plenty of salt and pepper. Bring to the boil, then turn down the heat and simmer the soup for 10 minutes.

4. Stir in the cream or buttermilk and the remaining tablespoon of Marsala or sherry. Taste the soup and adjust the seasoning as necessary. Fish out the dill frond.

5. For the garnish, heat the oil in a large frying pan. Add the mushrooms and sear them on both sides. Add the garlic and sprinkle over a pinch of allspice. Stir in half the herbs.

6. Serve the soup with the mushroom garnish, a sprinkling of the reserved herbs and the cream, if using.

Sausage & tortellini in brodo

SERVES 4

1 tbsp olive oil
4 meaty sausages, skinned
½ tsp fennel seeds (optional)
1 litre well-flavoured chicken
stock
300g small tortellini
75g cavolo nero, de-stemmed
and shredded
a few chilli flakes
salt and black pepper

TO SERVE
Parmesan shavings

I've been eating this for ever, and come on – sausage, chicken stock and tortellini in one bowl. Who's complaining? Surely nobody. It's good if you can buy fennel sausages for this, but if you can't find any, just use ordinary ones and add a few fennel seeds instead. Any flavour of tortellini is fine, such as ham and cheese or spinach and ricotta. And if you do have some lovely home-made chicken stock on hand that will be ace. You'll find our chicken stock recipe on page 273.

1. Heat the olive oil in a frying pan. Add the sausages and break them up a little in the pan with a wooden spoon. Cook, turning them over regularly, until well browned, then add the fennel seeds, if using, and cook for another minute.

2. Pour the chicken stock into a large saucepan and bring to the boil. Season with salt and pepper, then add the tortellini and cavolo nero. Cook until both are tender – this usually takes just a couple of minutes.

3. Drain the sausages on kitchen paper and divide between 4 bowls. Ladle over the broth, tortellini and cavolo nero, then sprinkle over a few chilli flakes. Serve with Parmesan to add at the table.

Halloumi & melon salad

SERVES 4

2 x 225g blocks of halloumi, cut into slices

1 tbsp olive oil

1 tsp dried mint

2 little gem lettuces, large leaves roughly chopped

1 orange-fleshed melon, peeled, deseeded and cut into chunks

seeds from ½ pomegranate

25g pumpkin seeds, lightly toasted

a few mint leaves

a few basil leaves

½ tsp sumac

DRESSING

2 tbsp olive oil

juice of ½ lemon

1 tsp sherry vinegar

salt and black pepper

Simple and fresh, this is a lovely dish for a light lunch or to serve as a side or starter. The salty halloumi and juicy melon make perfect partners and the pomegranate and pumpkin seeds add tang and crunch. Nice served with a hunk of good bread.

1. Toss the halloumi in the olive oil and dried mint. Heat a frying pan or griddle and brown the halloumi slices on both sides, then remove them from the pan and chop roughly.

2. Whisk the dressing ingredients together and season with salt and pepper.

3. Toss the lettuce in half the dressing and arrange it in a serving dish. Add the melon and halloumi, then sprinkle over the pomegranate and pumpkin seeds. Drizzle over the remaining dressing and finish with the herbs and a sprinkling of sumac.

Roasted potato & cauliflower salad

SERVES 4

3 tbsp olive oil
750g new/salad potatoes,
    halved or thickly sliced,
    blanched for 3 minutes.
1 small cauliflower, cut into
    small florets
1 red pepper, cut into strips
3 red chillies, sliced into
    rounds
1 tsp cumin seeds
50g walnuts, roughly chopped
150g spinach leaves
4 spring onions, roughly
    chopped
a few coriander leaves
a few mint leaves
½ tsp chilli flakes
salt and black pepper

DRESSING
2 tbsp tamarind purée
2 tbsp olive oil
1 tsp sesame oil
1 tsp hot sauce
about 2 tsp honey
juice of ½ lemon
1 garlic clove, crushed
1 tsp ground cumin
½ tsp ground cinnamon

RAITA
200ml yoghurt
1 tsp dried mint
zest of ½ lime
pinch of sugar

The potatoes and cauliflower in this veggie salad go so nicely together, particularly as they're both roasted. Then there's the earthy notes of the cumin and warmth of the cinnamon combined with the zesty punch of the tamarind – fantastic. I like to use the concentrated tamarind which is quite sour but really good in this salad. And don't forget the raita which adds a mellow note and balances all the flavours. This is a family favourite – and there's no sign of anything with legs!

1. Preheat the oven to 200°C/Fan 180°C/Gas 6. Put a roasting tin in the oven to heat up. Put 2 tablespoons of the olive oil into the tin, add the potatoes and season with salt. Roast in the oven for 20 minutes.

2. Add the cauliflower, pepper and chillies to the roasting tin. Drizzle over the rest of the olive oil and toss lightly to coat everything, then sprinkle over the cumin seeds. Add more salt and plenty of black pepper. Roast for another 20 minutes, adding the walnuts after 10 minutes, until the vegetables are all tender to the point of a knife.

3. Put all the dressing ingredients in a bowl and season with salt and pepper. Whisk together, then taste. Add a little more honey if you think it necessary, but bear in mind that the sourness of the tamarind will be balanced by the flavours in the rest of the salad and the raita.

4. To make the raita, mix the yoghurt, mint and lime zest together with a pinch of sugar and plenty of seasoning.

5. To assemble, divide the spinach and spring onions between 4 bowls. Add the roasted vegetables, then drizzle over some dressing and toss gently. Add the coriander and mint leaves and sprinkle with the chilli flakes. Serve with the raita and the rest of the dressing.

Beetroot, celery, orange & carrot salad with yuzu dressing

SERVES 4

6 small or 4 medium beetroots of similar size, preferably different colours, scrubbed
1 tbsp olive oil
a few thyme or rosemary sprigs
salt and black pepper

SALAD

2 oranges
100g salad leaves
1 large carrot, sliced into long ribbons
2 celery sticks, finely sliced, diagonally
250g soy beans, blanched, drained and refreshed in iced water
a few mint leaves, to garnish
a few coriander leaves, to garnish

DRESSING

2 tbsp olive oil
1 tsp sesame oil
1 tbsp dark soy sauce
1 tbsp Japanese rice vinegar
1 tbsp lemon or yuzu juice

Dave always liked to make salads like this with veg from his garden. Great at any time of year, this salad's fresh flavours are fantastic with barbecued pork or chicken and also work really well with barbecued celeriac steaks. Yuzu is a citrus fruit that's very popular in Japan and you can buy the juice in the UK now. If you like, though, you could use a bought ponzu sauce for the dressing instead of the soy, vinegar and citrus juice mixture.

1. Preheat the oven to 200°C/Fan 180°C/Gas 6. Put the beetroots in the centre of a large piece of foil and drizzle with the olive oil. Add the herbs and sprinkle generously with salt. Seal the foil into a parcel and place on a baking tray. Roast the beetroots for 45–60 minutes, depending on size, until they are knife tender.

2. Remove the beetroots from the oven and as soon as you can handle them, rub off the skins. Leave the beetroots to cool, then slice thinly, preferably with a mandoline.

3. Whisk the dressing ingredients together and season with salt and pepper.

4. Prepare the oranges. First, cut off the top and bottom of each one, so they can sit flat on your work surface, then cut away the rest of the skin, following the curve of the orange. Holding the orange over a bowl to catch the juice, cut out the segments, as close to the membrane as you can. Add any juice to the salad dressing.

5. To assemble, arrange the leaves over a large platter. Follow with the carrot ribbons, celery, soy beans, orange segments and beetroot slices. Drizzle over the dressing and garnish with the herbs.

Curried penne salad

300g penne pasta
2 tsp olive or sesame oil
1 cucumber, well chilled
2 tsp red wine vinegar
zest and juice of ½ lime

SAUCE
1 tbsp olive oil
1 onion, finely chopped
2 garlic cloves, finely chopped
5g root ginger, finely chopped
1 tsp nigella seeds
2 tsp curry powder
100ml chicken or vegetable
   stock
100ml double cream or
   yoghurt
salt and black pepper

TO SERVE
leaves from a few coriander
   sprigs, finely chopped
a few mint leaves
2 red chillies, sliced, or a few
   chilli flakes

The first time I had this was in an Italian family home. Italians are not known for fiddling with classic recipes, particularly when it comes to pasta, so imagine my surprise when I was faced with this salad! I have to say – this particular family was slightly avant garde, something that was reflected in their food. I thought this salad was flipping good and I've been making it for my family ever since.

1. Cook the penne in plenty of well-salted water, according to the packet instructions. Reserve a few ladlefuls of the cooking water for the sauce, then drain the pasta thoroughly. Toss it in the oil and leave to cool.

2. To make the sauce, heat the olive oil in a sauté pan. Add the onion and fry over a medium heat until soft and starting to colour. Stir in the garlic, ginger, nigella seeds and curry powder.

3. Add the stock, along with a ladleful of the reserved cooking water, then bring to the boil. Simmer until reduced by half, then add the double cream or yoghurt. Simmer very gently until you have a sauce that's the consistency of pourable double cream, then add the penne. Loosen with a little more of the cooking liquid if necessary and leave to cool.

4. To finish the salad, peel and deseed the cucumber, then slice it into fine crescents. Toss them in the vinegar, lime zest and juice. Season with salt and black pepper.

5. Toss the penne with the cucumber. Serve sprinkled with the coriander, mint leaves and chillies or chilli flakes.

Rice, artichoke & tuna salad

SERVES 4

400g cooked Camargue, black or wild rice
1 red onion, finely diced
100g tomatoes, diced, or cherry tomatoes, halved
1 small red pepper, finely diced
6 artichoke hearts from a jar or can, sliced
50g capers
25g cornichons, sliced
100g Gruyère cheese, finely diced
150g tuna from a jar or can, flaked
leaves from 2 large oregano sprigs, chopped
1 small bunch of parsley, finely chopped
½ tsp chilli flakes
75g salad leaves, roughly chopped
salt and black pepper

DRESSING
2 tbsp olive oil
juice and zest of 1 lemon
1 tbsp red wine vinegar

A proper main-course salad, this is dead simple to make and great to eat. Tuna and artichokes go so well together, particularly when served with black, red or wild rice. There's a nuttiness to these kinds of rice that really enhances a salad, but if you can only lay your hands on basmati this will still taste good.

1. Put the rice into a large bowl. Add the red onion, tomatoes, red pepper, artichoke hearts, capers, cornichons and Gruyère and mix thoroughly.

2. Whisk the dressing ingredients together and season with salt and pepper. Pour the dressing over the contents of the bowl and mix again.

3. Add the tuna, herbs and chilli flakes to the salad and gently fold them through – don't let the tuna break up too much.

4. Add the salad leaves just before serving.

Roasted Brussels sprouts & bacon salad

SERVES 4

500g Brussels sprouts, trimmed and halved

2 tbsp olive oil

½ tsp dried thyme

200g cooked puy, green or brown lentils

100g salad leaves (a mix with baby beetroot leaves or frisée works well)

75g radishes, halved and sliced

zest of ½ lemon

2 oranges, peel sliced off and flesh divided into segments (see p.94 for method)

25g hazelnuts, toasted and lightly broken up

1 tsp za'atar

BACON DRESSING

2 tbsp olive oil

150g bacon lardons (smoked or unsmoked)

2 shallots, finely sliced

2 tbsp sherry vinegar

1 tsp Dijon mustard

juice of ½ orange

OK, I can guess what you might be thinking, but please, suspend your disbelief as this is absolutely delicious. Clearly, if you're not a fan of Brussels sprouts it's a no-no, but if you do, this is the salad for you – so full of flavour, texture and nutritional goodness. It's a must.

1. Preheat the oven to 200°C/Fan 180°C/Gas 6. Put the Brussels sprouts in a roasting tin and drizzle them with the oil. Toss well to coat, then season with salt and pepper and sprinkle with the dried thyme. Roast the sprouts in the oven until they are lightly browned and their cores are tender. They should take 15–20 minutes depending on size, but give the sprouts a good shake after 10 minutes, then start checking for doneness after 15 minutes.

2. While the sprouts are roasting, make the dressing. Heat the olive oil in a small frying pan and add the bacon and shallots. Fry until the bacon is crisp, then add the sherry vinegar, mustard and orange juice. Whisk everything together and keep warm.

3. Arrange the lentils, salad leaves and radishes on a large platter or in 4 shallow bowls. Toss the Brussels sprouts in the lemon zest and add them to the salad. Drizzle over most of the dressing and toss lightly – just enough to let the dressing reach the leaves and lentils.

4. Top with the orange segments and hazelnuts and a final drizzle of the dressing, then finish with a sprinkling of za'atar. Serve warm.

Crispy duck salad

SERVES 4

4 heads of chicory, preferably
    red, finely shredded
½ a cucumber, cut into
    quarters lengthways and
    finely sliced
100g radishes, sliced into
    rounds
100g cherry tomatoes,
    quartered
4 spring onions, finely sliced
100g leftover duck meat,
    chopped
25g walnuts, lightly toasted
    and finely chopped
50g salad leaves (optional)
salt and black pepper

DRESSING
3 tbsp olive oil
1 tsp walnut or sesame oil
1 tbsp rice vinegar
1 tbsp dark soy sauce
2 tsp wholegrain mustard
2 tsp honey
10g root ginger, grated

If by any small miracle you have any leftovers after making Chinese duck pancakes (see page 198). this salad is right up your strada. Stickily delicious with lots of different flavours. the bitterness of the chicory is the perfect match for the sweetness of the duck. You could. of course, make this with some smoked duck or even leftover chicken.

1. Whisk all the dressing ingredients together, then taste and season with salt and black pepper. Leave the dressing to stand for at least half an hour so the flavour of the ginger has time to infuse the other ingredients.

2. Put the chicory, cucumber, radishes, cherry tomatoes and spring onions in a bowl with the duck meat, then season with salt and pepper. Pour over the dressing and stir to coat. Leave the salad to stand for 10 minutes, then garnish with the walnuts.

3. Serve the salad as it is or over salad leaves.

Warm Mediterranean beef salad

SERVES 4

500g bavette steak in 1 piece,
    at room temperature

SALAD

100g dried fregola
100g salad leaves, such as
    rocket and beetroot leaves
2 roasted red peppers, pulled
    into strips
150g tomatoes, roughly
    chopped
2 shallots, finely sliced
2 small courgettes, finely
    sliced
fresh oregano leaves
fresh parsley leaves
salt and black pepper

DRESSING

1 can of anchovies
50g sunblush tomatoes
    (preferably smoked but
    regular also fine)
1 tbsp olive oil (or use oil from
    the tomatoes)
3 garlic cloves, crushed
1 tsp dried oregano
½ tsp chilli flakes
1 tsp lemon zest
2 tsp balsamic vinegar

A gutsy main meal salad, this is full of Mediterranean flavours, topped off with a great anchovy dressing. Fregola are little balls of semolina pasta that are toasted to give a hint of nuttiness, but you could make this with flageolet beans if you prefer.

1. Take the meat out of the fridge at least an hour before you want to cook it, so it has time to come up to room temperature.

2. To cook the fregola, toast it briefly first in a pan – this really improves the flavour – then cook according to the packet instructions. Set aside.

3. Sprinkle the steak generously with salt. Heat a griddle pan (or a barbecue) until it's too hot to hold your hand over, then add the steak. Cook for several minutes, until a crust has developed and the steak lifts away from the griddle easily. Flip and continue to cook for several minutes until another crust has formed. Remove the steak from the pan and leave it to rest for at least 10 minutes. Slice across the grain and reserve any juices for the dressing.

4. To make the dressing, put the anchovies and their oil into a small food processor with the tomatoes and blitz to a smooth paste. Transfer to a small pan with the olive oil or oil from the tomatoes and add the garlic, oregano, chilli flakes and lemon zest. Heat gently to cook the garlic, then remove from the heat. Add the balsamic vinegar with a tablespoon of water and any of the meat juices, then mix well. Taste and adjust the seasoning as necessary.

5. Put the salad ingredients, including the fregola and half the herbs, in a large dish and drizzle over most of the dressing. Top with the beef and drizzle over the remaining dressing. Scatter with the reserved herbs.

Lamb & couscous salad

SERVES 4

SALAD

1 red onion, finely sliced

1 cucumber (see method)

100g salad leaves, such as lamb's lettuce

small bunch of mint, leaves only

small bunch of parsley, finely chopped

seeds from ½ pomegranate

salt

COUSCOUS

6 dried apricots, finely chopped

50ml freshly boiled water

pinch of saffron (optional)

100g couscous

½ tsp dried mint

zest of 1 lemon

1 tbsp olive oil

125ml tepid water

LAMB

1 tbsp olive oil

250g minced lamb

2 garlic cloves, finely chopped

½ tsp ground cinnamon

½ tsp dried mint

½ tsp dried oregano

1 tbsp tomato purée

1 tbsp harissa paste

salt and black pepper

DRESSING

3 tbsp olive oil

juice of 1 lemon

1 tbsp pomegranate molasses

1 tsp honey

Inspired by the trips Dave and I made to Morocco, this dish has all the wonderful flavours of North African cooking, such as apricot, saffron, dried mint and harissa. I know there are quite a few ingredients, but they all have their role and you'll be glad when you taste it. Another great main meal salad.

1. First start the salad. Put the red onion in a bowl and sprinkle with salt. Cover with cold water and leave to stand for half an hour. Halve the cucumber lengthways and deseed, then cut into crescents.

2. For the couscous, put the apricots in a large bowl, cover them with the 50ml of freshly boiled water and add the saffron, if using. Leave to stand until the apricots have softened and the water has been absorbed. Add the couscous, together with the mint, lemon zest and olive oil. Cover with 125ml of tepid water and cover the bowl with a plate. Leave to stand until the liquid has been absorbed, then fluff up the couscous with a fork and stir to combine with the apricots.

3. For the lamb, heat the olive oil in a large frying pan and add the lamb mince. Fry until well browned, then if the lamb has rendered out a lot of fat, drain some of this away. Add the garlic and stir for a minute or so, then add the remaining ingredients and season with salt and pepper. Add a splash of water and cook for a few minutes, stirring regularly, until the mixture smells intensely savoury.

4. To make the salad dressing, whisk everything together, then season with plenty of salt and pepper.

5. To assemble, arrange half the salad leaves over a large serving dish and sprinkle over the couscous. Add the remaining leaves and the cucumber, then drizzle over half the dressing. Sprinkle over the lamb, then top with the red onions, herbs and pomegranate seeds. Drizzle over more dressing before serving.

comfort classics

66 *When filming, our motto has always been: let's give it a go. What's the worst that can happen? The problem was that 50 per cent of the time the worst did happen. I remember us trying to cook crab soufflés on a charcoal grill on a 28ft boat in the middle of the churning Irish Sea. The soufflés ended up looking like beer mats. Dave said: 'Don't worry, they'll never show that.' But guess what – they did. In close-up.* 99

Cheese & onion puff pastry tart

SERVES 4

1 sheet of ready-rolled puff
    pastry
1 small egg, beaten
150g garlic and herb soft
    cheese, such as Boursin
    or similar
2 small red onions, very finely
    sliced
1 tsp caster sugar
2 tsp olive oil
leaves from 1 large thyme
    sprig
½ tsp chilli flakes
salt and black pepper

If you've got people coming round at short notice, look no further than this little tart of loveliness. Dave was always really good at rustling up this sort of thing – simple, quick and so delicious.

1. Preheat the oven to 200°C/Fan 180°C/Gas 6. Put a baking tray in the oven to heat up while you assemble the tart.

2. Unroll the pastry, leaving it on the parchment. Trim the parchment so there isn't too much overhang. Score a 1cm border all the way round the pastry, then brush the whole sheet with beaten egg.

3. Add the cheese to the remaining egg and mix together until smooth. The mixture may seem quite runny, but don't worry, it won't run off the tart.

4. Mix the red onions with half a teaspoon of salt, plenty of black pepper, the sugar and the olive oil.

5. Spread the egg and cheese mix over the pastry sheet, making sure it stops just shy of the scored border. Sprinkle over the onions, followed by the thyme leaves and chilli flakes.

6. Lift the tart on to the heated baking tray, then place it in the oven. Bake for 25–30 minutes until the pastry and the topping are golden and the onions have started to caramelise in places. Serve at once.

Potato, cheese & onion pie

SERVES 4

1kg potatoes, cut into chunks
2 onions, cut into quarters
1 tsp English mustard
75ml milk
50g butter
150g Cheddar, grated
2 medium tomatoes, sliced
½ tsp dried thyme
salt

This was one of my best mate's favourite things to eat. It reflects Dave's eating habits during his younger years and I think it is one of those recipes that sparks nostalgia and memories of a simpler world, of life at a slower pace.

1. Put the potatoes in a saucepan and cover them with water. Season with plenty of salt, then put the onions on top. Cover and bring to the boil, making sure you keep an eye on the pan, so the water doesn't boil over. Simmer, partially covered, for about 20 minutes until the potatoes and onions are tender.

2. Remove the onions from the pan and drain the potatoes. Mash the potatoes and beat in the mustard, milk and butter. Roughly chop the onions and stir them through the potato.

3. Preheat the oven to 200°C/Fan 180°C/Gas 6.

4. Pile the mash and onions into an ovenproof dish and sprinkle over the cheese. Arrange the tomato slices on top and sprinkle with the thyme.

5. Bake in the oven for about 20 minutes until the cheese has melted and started to brown. Nice with a salad.

Creamy mushroom pasta bake

SERVES 4

300g short-form pasta
1 tbsp olive oil
1 onion, finely chopped
400g mixed mushrooms, such
    as button and chestnut,
    thickly sliced
3 garlic cloves, finely chopped
leaves from a large thyme
    sprig
zest of ½ lemon
1 tsp porcini powder
    (optional)
100ml white wine
250g mascarpone cheese
100g baby leaf spinach
50g Parmesan, finely grated
200g Taleggio cheese
truffle oil (optional)
salt and black pepper

A simple favourite with both the King and Myers families, this is always tasty and always well received. Porcini powder is quite widely available now, but you can make your own by blitzing five grams of dried mushrooms to a powder.

1. Cook the pasta in plenty of salted boiling water. Set aside 200ml of the cooking water, then drain the pasta. Preheat the oven to 200°C/Fan 180°C/Gas 6.

2. While the pasta is cooking, heat the olive oil in a large sauté pan and add the onion. Fry until translucent and lightly coloured, then add the mushrooms. Fry them over a high heat until browned – if they give out any liquid, continue to cook until they are dry.

3. Stir in the garlic and cook for a minute, then add the thyme leaves, lemon zest and porcini powder, if using. Season with salt and black pepper and stir to combine.

4. Pour in the white wine. Bring to the boil and let it reduce down, then stir in the mascarpone. When it has melted into a sauce, add the reserved cooking water, a little at a time, until you have a sauce the consistency of single cream. Add the spinach, pushing it into the sauce until it has completely wilted down, then add half the Parmesan and the pasta. Stir again to combine.

5. Transfer everything to an ovenproof dish. Cut the Taleggio into slices and arrange them over the pasta. Top with the rest of the Parmesan.

6. Bake in the oven until the cheese has started to bubble and brown around the edges. For an extra touch of luxury, add a drizzle of truffle oil, if you have some, before serving.

White pizzas with smoked fish

MAKES 4 LARGE PIZZAS OR 6-8 SMALLER ONES

PIZZA DOUGH

500g strong white flour, plus extra for dusting
7g fast-acting dried yeast
1½ tsp salt
2 tbsp olive oil
300ml tepid water

TOPPING

250g crème fraiche or soured cream
250g cream cheese
2 x 125g balls of fresh mozzarella (drained weight), roughly torn
leaves from 2 large fresh oregano sprigs
2 tbsp capers
200g hot-smoked trout or salmon, roughly flaked
zest of 1 lemon
2 tsp olive oil
salt and black pepper

TO SERVE

60g rocket
1 tbsp olive oil
juice of ½ lemon

I do love a white pizza and I also love smoked fish. Put the two together and this recipe has to go down as one of my favourite comfort nibbles.

1. First make the pizza dough. Put the flour in a bowl with the yeast, mix thoroughly, then add the salt. Add the olive oil, then work in the tepid water and mix to form a dough. Leave to rest for half an hour.

2. Turn the dough out on to a floured work surface and knead until soft and elastic. This will probably take about 10 minutes.

3. Put the dough back in the bowl and cover with a damp tea towel. Leave it somewhere warm until it has roughly doubled in size. This should take about an hour but will depend on the ambient temperature.

4. Preheat the oven to its highest temperature and put 2 baking trays – or 4 if you have them – into the oven to heat up.

5. Divide the pizza dough into 4 equal pieces. Roll each piece as thin as you can – each should have a diameter of at least 30cm. Transfer each pizza base to a piece of baking parchment.

6. Mix the crème fraiche or soured cream with the cream cheese and spread the mixture over the 4 pizza bases. Top with the mozzarella, followed by the oregano and capers. Season with salt and pepper.

7. Put the pizzas in the hot oven for 7–10 minutes until lightly coloured and cooked through. Toss the fish in the lemon zest and olive oil, then arrange it over the pizzas. Put them back in the oven for another minute for the fish to heat through.

8. Season the rocket with salt and pepper and toss in the olive oil and lemon juice. Put a handful of leaves on top of each pizza and serve while hot.

Tuna savoury

SERVES 4

1 red onion, finely chopped
1 fat garlic clove, very finely
    chopped
zest and juice of ½ lime
2 celery sticks, finely chopped
50g cornichons, diced
25g capers, roughly chopped
2 cans of tuna fish (each about
    150g drained weight) or
    1 can of tuna, plus 150g
    chickpeas, roughly crushed
small bunch of parsley, finely
    chopped
50g mayonnaise
1 tbsp Dijon mustard
salt and black pepper

TO SERVE
4 large slices of sourdough
    or similar, toasted
1 garlic clove, cut in half
olive oil, for drizzling
4 medium tomatoes, sliced
    and drained
4 handfuls of salad leaves

Whether you're on the road or at home you can't beat a tuna savoury and as our Dave would say, this one's a belter. Great piled on toast, in a sandwich or as a topping for a baked potato. And if you're short on tuna, try substituting half the tuna with chickpeas. This makes things a bit cheaper and adds some healthy pulses to the dish.

1. Put the red onion in a large bowl with the garlic. Sprinkle with salt and add the lime zest and juice. Stir well and leave to stand for 15 minutes. Add the celery, cornichons, capers, tuna (or tuna and chickpeas), parsley, mayonnaise and mustard, then season and mix thoroughly.

2. Rub the toasted sourdough with the garlic and drizzle with olive oil. Add the tomatoes and season with salt and pepper. Add some salad leaves and pile the tuna mixture on top. Serve at once.

Stuffed potatoes with cheese & chorizo

SERVES 4

4 large baking potatoes
1 tbsp olive oil
15g butter
salt and black pepper

FILLING

1 tbsp olive oil
1 large onion, diced
75g cooking chorizo, diced
50g pitted green olives, sliced
2 garlic cloves, finely chopped
100g tomatoes, diced
1 tsp finely chopped lemon
    zest
1 small bunch of parsley, finely
    chopped
150g hard cheese, such as
    Manchego, mature Cheddar
    or Gruyère, grated

Now there are stuffed potatoes and then there are our stuffed potatoes. The filling is so flavoursome with a little bit of smokiness from the chorizo, big savoury hits from the cheese and olives and little pops of freshness from the tomatoes. Definitely a family fave.

1. First cook the potatoes. Preheat the oven to 200°C/Fan 180°C/Gas 6. Pierce the potatoes all over with a skewer, then rub them with olive oil and sprinkle with salt. Put them on a rack in the middle of the oven and bake for 1–1½ hours, depending on size. Alternatively, cook the potatoes in an air fryer or a microwave if you prefer.

2. Meanwhile, prepare the filling. Heat the olive oil in a large frying pan and add the onion. Sauté over a fairly high heat until the onion has softened and lightly browned – a bit of caramelisation is good. Add the chorizo and fry briskly until it has taken on some colour and rendered out some fat. Stir in the olives, garlic, tomatoes, lemon zest and half the parsley, then remove from the heat.

3. Remove the potatoes from the oven and cut them in half lengthways. Scoop out the potato flesh, leaving about ½cm still attached to the skins. Arrange the potato skins in an ovenproof dish – they should be quite a snug fit – and dot with butter. Season with salt and pepper.

4. Add the potato flesh and half the cheese to the contents of the frying pan. Stir to mix in the potatoes, then pile everything into the skins. Sprinkle with the remaining cheese and parsley.

5. Bake in the oven for another 15–20 minutes until the potatoes are piping hot and the cheese has melted and started to brown.

Full English breakfast pie

SERVES 4

1 x 500g block of all-butter puff pastry
plain flour, for dusting
1 small onion, finely chopped
100g bacon lardons
6 eggs
3 sausages, skinned
6 cherry tomatoes, halved
½ tsp oregano
2 tbsp ketchup or brown sauce
2 tsp hot sauce
dash of Worcestershire sauce
50g Cheddar, grated
salt and black pepper

Howay – that's Geordie for come on, obvs! What's not to love about this pie which has the bonus of puff pastry to propel your breakfast favourites into your gob. It's even got built-in ketchup or brown sauce and I promise it will make you very happy.

1. Preheat the oven to 200°C/Fan 180°C/Gas 6. Put a baking tray in the oven to heat up.

2. Cut the block of puff pastry into 2 pieces – one-third and two-thirds. Roll the larger piece out on a floured surface and use it to line a round pie dish – about 3cm deep and 20cm in diameter.

3. Mix the onion and bacon together and sprinkle them over the pastry. Crack 4 of the eggs and add them to the pie. Pierce the yolks with a knife tip and swirl them very slightly – you don't want the yolks and whites to combine, but the yolks do need to be broken up a bit. Season with a little salt and black pepper.

4. Beat the remaining 2 eggs in a bowl. Reserve 2 tablespoons for brushing the pie and pour the rest of the beaten egg into the pie.

5. Pinch off small balls, about the size of a large teaspoonful, from the sausages. Drop these into the eggs, spacing them as evenly as you can. Follow with the cherry tomatoes, making sure they are cut side up, and sprinkle over the oregano.

6. Mix the ketchup or brown sauce with the hot sauce and Worcestershire sauce. Drizzle the mixture over the pie, then sprinkle over the cheese.

7. Brush the pastry edges with the beaten egg. Roll out the remaining piece of pastry and use it to cover the pie. Crimp the edges together and brush the pie with more beaten egg. Cut 2 slits in the top of the pie.

8. Place on the heated baking tray and bake for 25–30 minutes until slightly puffed up, crisp and golden. Best served at room temperature.

Spicy lamb toasties

SERVES 4

1 tbsp olive oil

400g minced lamb (or 250g leftover roast lamb)

2 garlic cloves, finely chopped

1 tbsp Baharat spice

1 tsp chilli powder or hot sauce (optional)

1 tsp dried oregano

2 tbsp tomato purée

2 tsp red wine vinegar

½ tsp honey

3 spring onions, finely chopped

salt and black pepper

SANDWICHES

8 slices of bread (preferably sourdough)

butter, for spreading

2 cooked beetroots, thinly sliced

2 fat green or red chillies, finely sliced

2 roast red peppers, pulled into thick strips

200g mature Cheddar or similar, grated

When Dave and I first tasted Turkish lahmacun – spicy lamb on crisp flatbread – we hammered them and this recipe celebrates the memory of that moment. Instead of serving our spicy lamb on flatbread, we pile it into sandwiches which we then toast or fry. They are epic. Great with mince or with any leftover meat from the slow-roast lamb on page 212. I'm a big fan of Baharat, a blend of warm, smoky spices that's very popular in eastern Mediterranean and Middle Eastern cooking. It's available in large supermarkets.

1. Heat the olive oil in a frying pan and add the lamb. Fry over a high heat until well browned, then add the garlic, Baharat spice, chilli powder or hot sauce, if using, and the oregano. Stir for a minute, then add the tomato purée, vinegar and honey. Season with salt and pepper. Stir until the mixture smells intensely savoury, then stir in the spring onions.

2. Butter one side of each slice of bread. Divide the lamb between 4 of the slices, adding it to the unbuttered side, then top with the beetroot slices, chillies, peppers and cheese. Top with the remaining slices of bread – buttered side up.

3. Cook the sandwiches in a flat-plated toastie maker or fry them for several minutes on each side, pressing down firmly with a spatula to hold the sandwich together.

Corned beef poutine

GRAVY

1 tbsp beef dripping or olive oil

1 onion, very finely chopped

200g beef, finely diced or minced

1 tsp dried thyme

1 tsp garlic powder

1 tsp mustard powder

1 tbsp tomato purée

600ml well-flavoured beef stock or consommé

1 tsp Worcestershire sauce

salt and black pepper

TO SERVE

1 tbsp beef dripping or olive oil

200g corned beef, chilled and diced

1kg oven chips, cooked according to packet instructions, or 1kg home-made chips

75g Cheddar, grated

75g firm mozzarella, grated

chopped spring onions

fresh thyme leaves

A Canadian classic, poutine is the lumberjack version of loaded fries but with great flair and imagination. As you'd expect, Dave and I ate plenty of this when we travelled across Canada on a charity bike ride and we've cooked it loads at home since then. This is our latest version.

1. First make the gravy. Heat the beef dripping or olive oil in a saucepan and add the onion and beef. Fry over a high heat until the onion and beef are browned, then stir in the thyme, garlic and mustard powders and tomato purée. Stir to combine, then pour in the beef stock or consommé and the Worcestershire sauce. Season with salt and pepper, then stir to make sure the base of the pan is clean and nothing is sticking.

2. Bring to the boil, then turn down the heat and simmer for 20 minutes or so until you have a rich, slightly thickened gravy.

3. Heat the beef dripping or olive oil in a large frying pan. Fry the corned beef on all sides until crisp and lightly browned. Drain on kitchen paper, then add half the corned beef to the gravy.

4. Divide the cooked chips between 4 bowls. Mix the grated Cheddar and mozzarella together and sprinkle them over the chips. Ladle over the gravy, garnish with the rest of the corned beef and sprinkle with chopped spring onions and thyme leaves. Serve at once.

Beef curry hotpot

2 tbsp olive oil
20 curry leaves
1 tsp mustard seeds
1 large onion, finely sliced
15g root ginger, grated
4 garlic cloves, crushed
600g braising or stewing
    steak, diced
2 tbsp plain flour
2 tbsp tomato purée
1 tbsp curry powder
2 large carrots, sliced into
    rounds
500ml well-flavoured beef
    stock
1 tbsp HP sauce (optional)
salt and black pepper

POTATO TOPPING
25g butter
1 tsp cumin seeds
2 garlic cloves, finely chopped
2 green chillies, very finely
    sliced
800g floury potatoes, very
    thinly sliced (peeling
    optional)
100g Cheddar, grated
    (optional)
a few coriander sprigs, finely
    chopped

Well, you might remember that we came up with a cracking Indian shepherd's pie a while back and it was a big hit. So we thought to ourselves, why not a beef curry with a lovely potato topping? The curry hotpot was born! This is pure comfort and I know you're going to love it.

1. First make the beef curry. Heat the olive oil in a large, flameproof casserole dish, then add the curry leaves and mustard seeds. When they start crackling, add the onion and sauté until lightly golden and softening. Stir in the root ginger and garlic and cook for another couple of minutes.

2. Toss the pieces of steak with flour and season with salt. Dust off the excess, then add the meat to the casserole dish. Fry over a high heat until browned, then stir in the purée and curry powder. Add the carrots, then pour over the stock. Stir well to make sure the base of the casserole dish is clean and add the HP sauce, if using. Season with salt and pepper. Bring to the boil, then turn down the heat, cover the dish with a lid and leave the curry to simmer for half an hour.

3. While the beef is simmering, heat the butter for the topping in a small frying pan. Add the cumin seeds and cook for 30 seconds, then stir in the garlic and green chillies. Remove from the heat.

4. Remove the lid of the casserole dish and arrange the potato slices over the top. Season with salt and pour over the flavoured butter. Cover with a lid and leave to simmer for another 30 minutes or until the potatoes are just tender. Preheat the oven to 200°C/Fan 180°C/Gas 6.

5. Sprinkle the potatoes with the grated cheese, if using, as well as the coriander. Put the dish in the hot oven, uncovered, until the potatoes have crisped up and browned.

easy family suppers

66 For a long time, many of our fans thought that Dave and I lived together in sheltered accommodation with my mam. We'd try to set them straight, tell them about our wives, but we could usually see that they didn't believe us. One time I was with Dave and his wife Lil at a theatre and a lovely lady came up to us to say hello. Dave introduced her to Lil and the woman said to her: 'Ooh, it must be lovely living with them two. I bet you eat well!' 99

Tomato & courgette pasta

SERVES 4

400g short-form pasta
1 ball of mozzarella, finely
    diced
Parmesan shavings, to serve
    (optional)

TOMATO SAUCE
2 x 400g cans of peeled plum
    tomatoes (not chopped)
1 celery stick, roughly
    chopped
1 onion, halved
4 garlic cloves, lightly crushed
2 sage sprigs
25g butter
2 medium courgettes, very
    finely sliced
salt and black pepper

SAGE GARNISH (OPTIONAL)
2 tbsp olive oil
20 sage leaves
1 tbsp capers

Here's a quick and easy dish the whole family will love. An old Italian lady once said to me that Italians don't do fast food because what's easier than pasta? The sauce recipe makes more than you need, but I suggest you go ahead and do the full amount and save the rest for another dish. Small or medium courgettes are best for this, as they don't release too much liquid.

1. Put the tomatoes, celery, onion, garlic, sage and butter in a pan and season with salt and pepper. Rinse the cans out with 200ml of water and add this to the pan. Bring to the boil, then turn the heat down and leave the sauce to simmer very gently, uncovered, for about half an hour until everything is completely tender.

2. Remove the sage sprigs and purée the sauce until smooth. Reserve half the sauce for another time – it freezes well. Add the courgettes to the remaining sauce and continue to simmer until the courgettes are tender.

3. Cook the pasta in plenty of salted water, then drain. Add the pasta to the tomato sauce and stir to combine. Stir in the mozzarella at the last minute just before serving – that way it doesn't go stringy before you've managed to dish it up.

4. Make the garnish, if using. Heat the olive oil in a small frying pan and add the sage leaves and capers. Cook until the sage leaves are crisp – probably no longer than 30 seconds. Season with salt and use to garnish the pasta. Add a few Parmesan shavings, if using.

Aubergine stir-fry

SERVES 4

25g peanuts
3 tbsp vegetable oil
2 aubergines, cut into batons
1 large carrot, cut into
    matchsticks
10g root ginger, cut into fine
    matchsticks
3 garlic cloves, finely chopped
6 spring onions, whites and
    greens divided and finely
    sliced
large bunch of coriander,
    roughly chopped
100g kimchi, finely chopped

SAUCE
2 tsp gochujang
1 tbsp dark soy sauce
1 tbsp mirin
1 tsp cornflour
½ tsp honey or light brown
    sugar
½ tsp chilli powder (optional)
salt and black pepper

TO SERVE
4 nests of noodles, cooked
    according to the packet
    instructions
2 tsp dark soy sauce
½ tsp sesame oil

Actually, this is more like a cross between a stir-fry and a braise and is really great served over some noodles, as here, or with steamed rice. The meaty texture of the aubergines makes it a good, satisfying vegetarian dish. Try to find the slimmer, light purple aubergines if you can, as the skin is more tender and the shape is better for making batons. Only add the kimchi at the last minute and just gently warm it through to preserve its nutritional content.

1. First, mix all the sauce ingredients together, adding the chilli powder if you want extra heat. Season with salt and pepper, then stir in 100ml of water and set aside.

2. Heat a wok. Add the peanuts and toast them until aromatic, then remove them from the pan and leave to cool. Chop them roughly, then set aside.

3. Heat a tablespoon of the oil in the wok. Fry half the aubergines until browned on all sides, then remove and place on kitchen paper to drain. Repeat with another tablespoon of oil and the remaining aubergines.

4. Add the remaining oil to the wok, then add the carrot and ginger and stir-fry for a couple of minutes. Add the garlic and the spring onion whites and stir-fry for a further couple of minutes.

5. Pour the sauce into the wok, then add the aubergines and stir gently to coat them with the sauce. Simmer until the aubergines are tender and the sauce has reduced around them. Add a splash of water if the sauce reduces too much before the aubergines have softened.

6. Stir in the coriander, followed by the kimchi. Leave the wok to stand over a low heat for a minute, just so everything is brought up to temperature.

7. Toss the noodles in the soy and sesame oil, then divide them between 4 bowls. Add the contents of the wok, then finish with a sprinkling of the chopped toasted peanuts and the spring onion greens.

Spring vegetable & goat's cheese tray bake

SERVES 4

1 fennel bulb, trimmed and cut
into 8 wedges

3 slender leeks, cut into 5cm
lengths

750g baby new potatoes,
blanched for 5 minutes
in salted water

a few garlic cloves, left unpeeled

2 tbsp olive oil

100ml white wine

2 large tarragon sprigs, roughly
torn, plus leaves from 1 more
sprig, finely chopped

2 courgettes, thickly sliced

150g asparagus tips

2 little gem lettuces, halved

2 small, ripe goat's cheeses with
rind

grating of lemon zest

a few lemon thyme or thyme
leaves

salt and black pepper

Everyone loves a tray bake. This one is quick to prepare, fresh tasting and the goat's cheese makes it a little different. It's a texture thing – gooey, savoury loveliness.

1. Preheat the oven to 200°C/Fan 180°C/Gas 6.

2. Put the fennel, leeks and potatoes into a large roasting tin with the garlic cloves. Drizzle over half the olive oil and mix, then pour in the white wine with 100ml of water and add the roughly torn tarragon sprigs. Roast in the oven for about 35 minutes.

3. Toss the courgettes, asparagus tips and little gems in the remaining olive oil and the finely chopped tarragon, then add them to the roasting tin. Roast for a further 10 minutes.

4. Cut each goat's cheese horizontally through the middle, so you have 4 rounds, then place them in the roasting tin, rind side down. Sprinkle over some lemon zest and add the lemon thyme or thyme leaves. Season with salt and pepper.

5. Bake in the oven for another 5 minutes, until the cheese has melted.

Carlin pea, squash & spinach curry

SERVES 4

2 tbsp coconut oil
1 tsp cumin seeds
1 tsp mustard seeds
1 onion, diced
3 garlic cloves, crushed
  or grated
15g root ginger, grated
1 tbsp curry powder
1 tsp chilli powder
500g cooked carlin peas
  (see p.42) or 2 x 400g cans,
  drained)
300g butternut squash, diced
750g frozen whole leaf
  spinach, defrosted and
  drained
400ml can of coconut milk
200ml vegetable stock
200g cherry tomatoes, halved
  if large
salt and black pepper

TO SERVE
squeeze of lime juice
fresh coriander
sliced green chillies

Carlin peas are a much underused and underrated pulse – take a look at page 42 for more info about them. They are delicious and full of nutty, earthy flavour and when paired with the sweet squash, spinach and spice, they make a great veggie curry. A word of warning – this may lead to a little flatulence but so worth it.

1. Heat the coconut oil in a large saucepan or a flameproof casserole dish. Add the cumin and mustard seeds. When the seeds start spitting, add the onion and continue to cook over a medium-high heat until the onion has started to take on some colour. Add the garlic, ginger and spices and cook for another couple of minutes.

2. Add the carlin peas and butternut squash. Stir to coat them in the spices, then add the spinach, coconut milk and stock. Stir well and make sure nothing is catching on the base of the pan, then season generously with salt and pepper.

3. Bring to the boil, then turn the heat down to a simmer. Continue to cook, uncovered, and keep stirring regularly until the coconut and spinach have thickened into a rich sauce around the squash and peas.

4. Add the cherry tomatoes and cook for a few minutes until they have softened and are close to bursting if whole. Taste the curry and adjust the seasoning as necessary.

5. Finish with a squeeze of lime juice and serve with plenty of fresh coriander and green chillies for extra heat.

Cannellini bean bake

SERVES 4

2 tbsp olive oil
1 onion, very finely chopped
1 small fennel bulb, finely
    chopped
3 garlic cloves, finely chopped
2 rosemary sprigs, finely
    chopped
300g slender green beans,
    trimmed
1 large courgette, finely sliced
150ml white wine
300g fresh tomatoes, puréed
2 x 400g cans of cannellini
    beans in salted water,
    drained
zest of ½ lemon
small bunch of parsley, finely
    chopped
salt and black pepper

TOPPING
1 tbsp olive oil
100g dried breadcrumbs
25g Parmesan, finely grated
zest of ½ lemon

A soothing and nourishing supper dish that'll please the vegetarians in your family. If you leave out the Parmesan, this can be vegan too. I find it best to use beans canned in salted water for dishes like this where you want the beans to retain their shape. The salt helps the texture of the beans and stops them going mushy. Nice with a crisp green salad.

1. Heat the olive oil in a large flameproof casserole dish or an ovenproof sauté pan. Add the onion and fennel and sauté until they are translucent.

2. Add the garlic, rosemary, green beans and courgette, stir for a couple of minutes, then pour in the white wine. Season with salt and pepper, then cover the pan and leave to simmer for 10–15 minutes or so until the vegetables are very tender.

3. Add the tomatoes, cannellini beans, lemon zest and most of the chopped parsley – set aside 2 tablespoons for the topping. Bring to the boil, then turn the heat down to a simmer and cook for about 10 minutes.

4. Preheat the oven to 200°C/Fan 180°C/Gas 6. To prepare the topping, heat the olive oil in a small pan and add the breadcrumbs. Stir until they are well coated and starting to colour, then remove from the heat and leave to cool. Season with salt and pepper, then add the Parmesan, lemon zest and reserved parsley.

5. Sprinkle the topping over the beans, then put the dish in the oven for 15–20 minutes until bubbling and lightly golden.

TIP
This dish doesn't have to be baked if you want to save on fuel. Just fry the breadcrumbs for a little longer than above, until golden, and cook the beans for another 5 minutes, uncovered, to reduce a little. Sprinkle over the topping as it is or put the dish under the grill for 5 minutes.

Crisp omelette

SERVES 2–4

1 tbsp olive oil
1 small onion, very finely
    chopped
6 eggs, well beaten
100g cheese and onion crisps
4 slices of Serrano ham,
    shredded or pulled into
    strips
50g Manchego cheese, diced
1 tbsp finely chopped parsley,
    to serve
salt

Cheese and onion crisps are a culinary masterpiece in my opinion and when they're added to an omelette along with a little bit of Serrano ham – now you're talking. Dave and I have always loved a crisp and take any excuse to eat them – including making this recipe, which has always gone down a treat with both our families.

1. Heat the oil in an omelette pan and add the onion. Fry over a medium-high heat until the onion has started to lightly brown and crisp – you just want to take the edge off the rawness, not cook the onion completely.

2. Put the eggs in a bowl with a generous pinch of salt and beat until frothy. Add all but a small handful of the crisps and push them into the eggs. Leave to stand for a minute so that the crisps soften a bit.

3. Sprinkle half the ham and cheese over the onions, then pour in the eggs. Make sure the crisps are pushed into the eggs – you don't want air pockets forming. Add the remaining ham and cheese and cook until the underside is just cooked but not coloured – this should take 4–5 minutes.

4. Take a large plate and place it over the omelette pan. Upturn the pan so the omelette falls on to the plate, then slide it straight back into the pan for another couple of minutes to cook the underside. (If you don't want to flip the omelette, put it under the grill for a few moments instead.)

5. Slide the omelette out on to a clean plate and cut into halves or quarters. Crumble up the rest of the crisps and sprinkle them over the omelette, then top with the chopped parsley and serve. A tomato salad makes a good accompaniment.

Blackened fish with pineapple salsa

SERVES 4

4 thick fish fillets, such as cod,
    haddock, snapper
    or redfish, skinned
2 tbsp olive oil
salt and black pepper

MARINADE (OPTIONAL)
½ small onion
2 garlic cloves
1 scotch bonnet
zest of 1 lime

SALSA
250g fresh pineapple, diced
2 spring onions, finely sliced
leaves from a thyme sprig
a few basil leaves, shredded
zest and juice of ½ lime
½ scotch bonnet, very finely
    chopped (optional)
2 tsp red wine vinegar

RUB
1 tbsp plain flour
1 tsp mustard powder
1 tsp garlic powder
1 tsp ground cumin
1 tsp dried oregano
½ tsp chilli powder
½ tsp ground cinnamon
½ tsp ground allspice

TO SERVE (OPTIONAL)
rice and peas (see p.260)

I just love this Caribbean-inspired dish. We've said that the marinade is optional, but please do it if you have time, as it really helps the texture and flavour of the fish. If you feel like having something a bit different, try this. It's a goody.

1. If you have time, marinate the fish. Put the ingredients for the marinade in a small food processor with 50ml of water and blitz, then add plenty of salt. Tip the marinade into a bowl, add the fish fillets and leave for at least half an hour.

2. To make the salsa, mix everything together in a bowl and season with plenty of salt and black pepper.

3. To make the rub, put all the ingredients in a bowl and add half a teaspoon of salt and plenty of black pepper. Remove the fish from the marinade and pat it dry. Dip the fish into the rub, making sure it is well covered.

4. Heat the olive oil in a large frying pan. Add the fish and fry it on one side until a brown crust has developed and it lifts cleanly off the pan. You should be able to see that it has cooked at least halfway up the side. Flip over and cook for another couple of minutes.

5. Serve with the salsa and some rice and peas if you like.

Poached white fish in a cream & herb sauce

3 tarragon sprigs, bruised
3 parsley sprigs, bruised
100ml white wine
200ml fish stock
4 white fish fillets, skinned
    unless very thin
salt and black pepper

SAUCE
50g butter
1 shallot, very finely chopped
150ml poaching liquor
75ml double cream
1 tbsp finely chopped
    tarragon
1 tbsp finely chopped parsley
a few lemon thyme leaves
    (optional)

GARNISH
150g broad beans (about 500g
    in their pods and shells)
1 tbsp olive oil
50g capers
lemon zest

A bit of a classic this one and there are numerous variations on the theme, but here is our favourite. The tarragon in the creamy sauce works beautifully with the fish and I love the broad bean garnish.

1. First prepare the broad beans for the garnish. Blanch them in boiling water for just 1 minute, then refresh under cold water. Slip off the greyish outer skins, then set the beans aside until almost ready to serve.

2. Put the sprigs of tarragon and parsley in a wide, lidded sauté pan, add the wine and stock, then bring to the boil. Season the fish fillets with salt and pepper and lower them into the poaching liquor. Turn down the heat and cover the pan, then leave to simmer very gently until just cooked through. This should take about 5 minutes, but will depend on the thickness of the fish.

3. When the fish is cooked, remove the pan from the heat and ladle off most of the poaching liquor for the sauce. Cover the pan and leave the fish to keep warm in just a little of the liquid.

4. Start the sauce while the fish is cooking. Melt the butter in a pan, add the shallot and cook very gently until softened. Once the fish is done, add the poaching liquor to the pan with the shallot and bring to the boil. Simmer until the liquor has reduced by a third, then add the cream and continue to simmer until the sauce is reduced. Taste for seasoning, then stir in the herbs.

5. To finish the garnish, heat the olive oil in a small frying pan and add the double-podded broad beans and the capers. Fry over a high heat for just 30 seconds, then stir in the lemon zest.

6. Carefully remove the fish from the pan and place on warm plates. Spoon over some of the sauce. Garnish with the broad beans and capers, then grate over a little more lemon zest and serve with a green vegetable.

Sardine linguine

SERVES 4

500g linguine
100g rocket, spinach or salad
    leaves (optional)
salt and black pepper

SAUCE
2 cans of sardines (84g
    drained weight or similar)
    in olive oil
1 red onion, very finely
    chopped
2 garlic cloves, finely chopped
½ tsp fennel seeds
½ tsp dried thyme
½ tsp chilli flakes
zest of 1 lemon
3 tbsp tomato purée
3 tbsp capers
1 lemon

Canned sardines are cheap and really good for you, as they are full of omega-3 and so, so tasty. And who doesn't have a can of sardines in their store cupboard? This recipe takes me back to filming our very first telly episode in Portugal when Dave and I ate loads of sardines, both canned and fresh.

1. First get the pasta started. Bring a large saucepan to the boil (it boils faster if you put the lid on, but you know that), then add a handful of salt. Add the pasta and cook until just al dente, then add the greens which should wilt immediately in the liquid. Reserve a few ladlefuls of the cooking water, then drain.

2. Meanwhile, make the sauce. Drain the oil from the sardines into a frying pan and heat. Add the sardines and fry them briefly on both sides, then remove them from the pan and set aside.

3. Add the onion and sauté until starting to soften. Stir in the garlic, fennel seeds, thyme, chilli flakes, lemon zest and tomato purée. Stir to combine for a minute, then add a couple of ladlefuls of the pasta cooking water to make a sauce.

4. Bring the sauce to the boil and simmer for a couple of minutes, then add a little more of the cooking liquid if you think it needs it – the consistency should be pourable but not too thin.

5. Put the sardines back in the pan and add the capers. Add the pasta and greens and toss everything together. Serve with a generous squeeze of lemon juice.

Hake with salsa verde

4 hake steaks (or other white
 fish)
2 tbsp olive oil
zest of ½ lemon
15g butter
1 garlic clove, finely chopped

SALSA VERDE
1 large bunch of parsley
leaves from a small bunch
 of tarragon
leaves from a large thyme
 sprig
a few basil leaves
25g capers
juice of 1 lemon
2 tsp sherry vinegar
1 tbsp mustard
75ml olive oil
salt and black pepper

*Dave and I have always been massive fans of hake and we've often
enjoyed it in Spain where it's enormously popular. Here, served with
salsa verde, it's a great example of simple is best.*

1. First make the salsa verde. Chop the herbs and capers together as finely
as you can, put them in a bowl and season with salt and pepper. Add the
lemon juice, along with the sherry vinegar, then gradually work in the
mustard and olive oil. Taste and adjust as necessary – you might need
a little more vinegar. Set aside.

2. Remove the fish from the fridge at least half an hour before you want to
start cooking, so it is coming up to room temperature. Mix a tablespoon
of the olive oil with the lemon zest and rub this over the fish.

3. Heat the remaining olive oil in a large frying pan. Add the hake steaks and
cook them over a high heat for 3–4 minutes, then flip them over and cook
for another couple of minutes. Add the butter and when it has melted
and foamed around the fish, add the garlic and cook it very briefly.

4. Serve the fish with the garlicky butter spooned over and plenty of the
salsa verde.

Tagliatelle with pancetta & peas

SERVES 4

400g tagliatelle
1 tbsp olive oil
1 onion, finely chopped
100g pancetta, finely diced
3 garlic cloves, finely chopped
15g butter
250g fresh or frozen peas,
    blanched for 1 minute if
    fresh
100ml double cream
50g Parmesan, finely grated
salt and black pepper

Quick, simple, delicious, this is a great favourite in both our homes. It's a really satisfying supper and kids love it. In this recipe, we take the authentic Italian approach to many pasta dishes which is to use some of the pasta cooking water in the sauce. It's full of good starch which thickens the sauce and adds texture and flavour.

1. Cook the tagliatelle in plenty of salted, boiling water until just al dente. Reserve 3 ladlefuls (about 200ml) of the cooking water before straining the pasta and set them aside.

2. While the pasta is cooking, start the sauce. Heat the olive oil in a large sauté pan and add the onion and pancetta. Fry over a medium heat until the onion has softened and the pancetta is crisp and brown. Stir in the garlic and cook for another minute.

3. Add the butter and the peas and swirl them about until the butter has melted. Add 2 ladlefuls of the reserved cooking liquid from the pasta and season with salt and pepper. Bring to the boil and simmer for a few minutes until the sauce has reduced a little, then pour in the double cream. Simmer until the sauce is piping hot and slightly reduced.

4. Add the pasta to the sauté pan and stir until coated with the sauce. If the sauce seems a bit on the thick side, add a little more of the cooking water and simmer for another minute.

5. Serve with plenty of Parmesan and black pepper.

Chicken braised with grapes & new potatoes

SERVES 4

1 tbsp olive oil

15g butter

4 chicken legs

1 onion, thickly sliced

4 garlic cloves, finely chopped

100ml white wine

leaves from a large oregano sprig

750g baby new potatoes

300ml chicken stock

2 tsp Dijon mustard

24 red grapes

1 tbsp crème fraiche

salt and black pepper

This is a take on Italian mostarda – a northern Italian treat made of candied fruit and a mustard-flavoured syrup, often served with boiled meats or with cheese. We've taken those flavours of sweet fruit and mustard to use in our chicken braise to make a good supper for all.

1. Heat the olive oil and butter in a large flameproof casserole dish or a lidded sauté pan. Season the chicken with salt, then sear it, skin-side down, until the skin is nicely browned and crisp. Turn the chicken legs over and brown them on the other side, then remove them from the pan and set aside.

2. Add the onion and sauté until it's starting to turn translucent, then stir in the garlic and cook for a further minute. Pour in the white wine and allow it to bubble up, stirring to make sure the base of the pan is deglazed.

3. Put the chicken back in the pan. Add the oregano leaves, then tuck the potatoes in around the chicken. Add the chicken stock and mustard and season with salt and pepper.

4. Bring to the boil, then partially cover the pan and turn down the heat. Leave to simmer for about 20–25 minutes until the chicken is cooked through and the potatoes are tender.

5. Add the grapes and crème fraiche to the pan and simmer gently for another 5 minutes, uncovered, so the sauce reduces down a little. Serve with a green salad or some steamed greens.

Bacon chop schnitzels

SERVES 4

4 smoked bacon chops, off
    the bone
2 tbsp plain flour
1 tsp dried sage
1 egg
1 tsp Worcestershire sauce
50g fine dried breadcrumbs
2 tbsp olive oil
salt and black pepper

TO SERVE
450g spinach, well washed
10g butter
a grating of nutmeg
4 eggs, poached or fried

What a little wonder this recipe is. Dave always loved a bacon chop and here they are. dressed to the nines. Think of this as a fabulous new way to enjoy bacon and eggs. Perhaps it's the new Full English? You could also use bacon or gammon steaks for this recipe.

1. Trim the bacon chops of any excess fat. Place a chop between 2 pieces of cling film and bash with a mallet or rolling pin until very thin – less than ½cm thick. Repeat with the rest of the chops.

2. Sprinkle the plain flour over a plate and season with salt and pepper. Mix in the sage. Break the egg into a shallow bowl and beat with the Worcestershire sauce. Pour the breadcrumbs on to another plate.

3. Dip each bacon chop in the seasoned flour and tap off any excess. Dip it in the egg mixture, then coat in the breadcrumbs.

4. Heat the olive oil in a large frying pan and fry the schnitzels on both sides until crisp and golden brown – they will cook through very quickly. Transfer to a plate and keep warm.

5. Push the spinach into a large saucepan and heat until it wilts down. Season with salt and pepper, then drain. Toss in the butter and sprinkle over a little nutmeg.

6. Serve the schnitzels on a bed of wilted spinach and top each serving with a poached or fried egg.

Sausage & red wine risotto

SERVES 4

1 tbsp olive oil

15g butter

1 red onion, finely chopped

4 large sausages, skinned and crumbled

3 garlic cloves, finely chopped

leaves from 1 thyme sprig

300g risotto rice

150ml red wine

2 tbsp tomato purée

1 litre chicken stock, warmed through

TO FINISH

25g butter

25g Parmesan, grated, plus more for grating

A northern Italian classic, the addition of red wine here instead of the usual white, gives this risotto a lovely rich deep colour. A beautifully winning warmer and one of Dave's favourites.

1. Heat the olive oil in a large sauté pan. Add the butter and when it has melted, add the red onion and crumbled sausages. Cook, stirring regularly, until the onion is translucent and the sausage is well browned.

2. Add the garlic, thyme and rice and stir until the rice is glossy with the oil and butter. Pour in the red wine. Turn up the heat and allow the wine to bubble furiously around the rice. When most of the wine has boiled off, stir in the tomato purée and season with a little salt and pepper.

3. Start adding the stock, a ladleful at a time. When each ladleful of stock has been absorbed by the rice, add more, until you have used it all up and the rice is suspended in a rich, creamy sauce. The texture of the rice should be very slightly al dente and when you pull a spoon along the base of the pan, the rice should slowly fall back into its wake.

4. Beat in the butter and Parmesan, then serve the risotto with more Parmesan to add at the table.

Sriracha pork with noodles

SERVES 4

4 pork chops, on the bone
4 bundles of flat rice noodles
½ small red or pointed green
    cabbage, finely shredded
1 large carrot, finely shredded
1 red pepper, finely shredded
4 spring onions, finely
    chopped
1 small bunch of coriander,
    roughly chopped
leaves from 1 small bunch
    of mint
1 tsp sesame seeds
salt

MARINADE
1 tbsp sriracha
1 tbsp dark soy sauce
zest and juice of ½ lime
2 garlic cloves, crushed
1 tbsp mirin
2 tsp honey
1 tbsp sesame oil

DRESSING
2 tsp sesame oil
1 tsp crushed chillies, plus
    extra to serve
1 tbsp dark soy sauce
zest and juice of ½ lime
1 tbsp rice wine vinegar
½ tsp honey

The humble pork chop has never looked and tasted so good. The marinade is a wonderful mix of spicy, zesty, savoury and sweet, while the bed of noodles is fresh and crisp and the dressing has a little heat and a touch of sourness. You do need to allow a little time to marinate the meat and soak the cabbage and carrot, but once this is done, it's all quick to cook. Enjoy.

1. Mix the marinade ingredients together. Put the pork chops in a bowl, season them with salt, then cover them with the marinade. Leave them to stand for at least half an hour.

2. Cook the noodles according to the packet instructions. This usually involves soaking them in freshly boiled water for 3–4 minutes until soft. Drain and refresh under cold water.

3. Put the cabbage and carrot in a colander and sprinkle with salt. Leave to drain over a bowl for half an hour.

4. Whisk the dressing ingredients together and taste, then adjust the flavours as you like.

5. Heat a large griddle or frying pan. Scrape most of the marinade off the pork chops and place them on the pan. Cook for 3–4 minutes until char lines have appeared and the chops pull away from the pan cleanly. Turn the chops over and baste the cooked side with the marinade. Cook for another 3–4 minutes, then turn and baste again. Cook each side for another couple of minutes, continuing to baste. Remove the chops from the pan and leave them to rest for a few minutes.

6. To assemble, toss the noodles with the cabbage and carrot, red pepper, spring onions, herbs and the dressing. Top with the pork chops, then sprinkle with sesame seeds. Serve with more crushed chillies at the table.

Sausage, fennel & white wine casserole

SERVES 4

2 tbsp olive oil
2 fennel bulbs, cut into
  wedges
8 meaty sausages
3 garlic cloves, finely chopped
100ml white wine
400ml chicken or vegetable
  stock
1 tbsp wholegrain mustard
1 piece of pared lemon zest
½ tsp chilli flakes
1 large thyme sprig
1 large tarragon sprig
750g new potatoes, skin on,
  halved if large
100g baby broad beans
  (podded weight)
2 leeks, cut into thick rounds
2 courgettes, cut into slices
2 tbsp crème fraiche
  (optional)
small bunch of parsley, finely
  chopped
salt and black pepper

Dave and I have always loved a sausage and we enjoyed coming up with recipes to elevate this humble ingredient above its station. We think this dish does the trick. With the white wine and lots of vegetables, it's a lighter, more summery sausage casserole than usual. A cracking dish.

1. Heat half the olive oil in a large flameproof casserole dish. Add the fennel wedges and sear them on the cut sides. Remove the fennel and set aside, then add the remaining olive oil and the sausages. Brown the sausages on all sides, then add the garlic and cook for a further minute.

2. Pour in the white wine and bring to the boil, while stirring to scrape up any brown bits sticking to the base of the casserole dish. Add the stock, mustard, lemon zest, chilli flakes and herbs, followed by the potatoes and seared fennel. Season with salt and pepper.

3. Bring everything to the boil again, then turn down the heat. Partially cover the pan and leave to simmer for 20 minutes. Add the broad beans, leeks and courgettes and continue to cook for another 10 minutes or so until everything is tender.

4. Stir in the crème fraiche, if using, and leave to simmer for another couple of minutes.

5. Serve in large shallow bowls, with a sprinkling of parsley and perhaps some bread on the side.

relax,
it's the
weekend

66 We've spent so much time travelling the world over the last twenty or so years and great though it's been, Dave and I always loved a bit of normal downtime. Exotic locations are all very well, but for us, there was nothing better than hunkering down in the back garden with a few mates and a beer or two, listening to some favourite tracks while the barbecue fired up. We'd have some burgers, lamb ribs and chicken in a nice marinade ready and waiting. 99

Stuffed butternut squash

SERVES 4

1 large butternut squash
(or 2 small ones), halved
and seeds scooped out

1 tbsp olive oil

1 garlic clove, halved

a few rosemary sprigs

salt and black pepper

FILLING

2 tbsp olive oil

1 small onion, finely chopped

1 celery stick, finely chopped

2 garlic cloves, finely chopped

1 tsp dried sage

small bunch of parsley, chopped

zest of 1 lemon

½ tsp ground cinnamon

50g sunblush tomatoes, chopped

400g can of butter beans, drained

25g pecans, roughly chopped

½ block of halloumi (about 100g),
coarsely grated

Dave loved to grow all sorts of vegetables in his garden, including the wonder that is the butternut squash. Here's a real showpiece of a recipe to treat your vegetarian family members and friends. It looks spectacular and tastes great.

1. Preheat the oven to 200°C/Fan 180°C/Gas 6. Put the squash halves in a roasting tin. Score the flesh of the squash in a criss-cross pattern, stopping short of the skin. Rub with the olive oil, followed by the garlic, then arrange the rosemary over the top. Season with salt and pepper.

2. Roast the squash in the oven for 35–40 minutes or until the flesh is just tender. Remove from the oven and discard the rosemary sprigs. Scoop out most of the squash flesh, leaving a 1cm thick shell. Finely chop the flesh and set it aside.

3. To make the filling, heat half the oil in a saucepan. Add the onion and celery and sauté until soft and translucent, then stir in the garlic and cook for another 2 minutes. Add them to the squash flesh, then stir in the herbs, lemon zest, cinnamon, sunblush tomatoes, butter beans, pecans and half the cheese. Season with a little salt (you won't need much, as the halloumi is quite salty) and black pepper.

4. Pile the filling into the squash halves, pushing it down as much as you can manage – it will create quite a mound on top. Sprinkle with the remaining cheese and drizzle with the rest of the olive oil.

5. Bake in the oven for a further 10–15 minutes until the filling is piping hot and the cheese has lightly browned.

Broccoli & cheese quiche

SERVES 4

200g long-stemmed broccoli
5 eggs, lightly beaten
200ml double cream
125ml crème fraiche
leaves from a large tarragon
 sprig, finely chopped
1 tbsp Dijon or tarragon
 mustard (optional)
1 small onion, finely chopped
150g cheese (Gruyère, Comté,
 Cheddar are all good),
 grated
salt and black pepper

PASTRY
250g plain flour, plus extra for
 dusting
125g butter, chilled and diced
1 egg yolk
iced water

What is it about quiche? People either love it or hate it. The problem is that it's so often as dry and stodgy as a sergeant major's insole, but when it's made properly, there's no finer dish. Make this and rediscover how great a quiche can be.

1. First make the pastry. Put the flour in a bowl and add half a teaspoon of salt. Add the butter and rub it in until the mixture resembles fine breadcrumbs. Using a table knife, mix in the egg yolk, then add a little iced water, a teaspoon at a time, until the mixture comes together into a dough. You can, of course, do all this in a food processor.

2. Form the pastry into a ball. Roll it out on a floured surface and use it to line a 28cm round flan tin. Cut off any overhanging pastry, but don't trim too much – it's better to do this after it has been cooked. Chill for at least half an hour or freeze for 10 minutes.

3. Preheat the oven to 200°C/Fan 180°C/Gas 6. Line the pastry case with parchment and add baking beans. Bake in the oven for 15–20 minutes until the pastry has set and is starting to take on some colour. Remove the parchment and beans and put the pastry back in the oven for a further 5 minutes. Remove from the oven and leave to cool. Turn the oven down to 160°C/Fan 140°C/Gas 3.

4. For the filling, steam the broccoli for 3–4 minutes until it's knife tender. Refresh under cold water.

5. Put the eggs in the bowl with the cream and crème fraiche and season with salt and pepper. Whisk very gently to combine, trying to avoid getting too much air into the mixture – the less air, the smoother the set will be. If any froth forms, leave the mixture to stand until it has subsided. Stir in the tarragon.

6. Spread the mustard, if using, over the base of the pastry case. Sprinkle over the onion and half the cheese, followed by the broccoli. Carefully pour over the egg mixture, then sprinkle over the remaining cheese.

7. Bake the quiche in the oven for 35–40 minutes until just set – it should have a slight wobble. Remove from the oven and leave to cool for a few minutes before serving. Best eaten warm or at room temperature.

Aubergine & black bean burgers

SERVES 6

1 large aubergine, cut in half lengthways
1 red onion, cut into wedges
1 tsp dried mixed herbs
2 tbsp olive oil, plus more for brushing
4 garlic cloves, unpeeled
2 x 400g cans of black beans, drained (or 500g cooked black beans)
100g breadcrumbs
1 tsp cumin seeds
2 tbsp sesame seeds
1 tbsp tomato purée
2 tsp chipotle paste
salt and black pepper

CHIPOTLE MAYO
100ml mayonnaise
2 tsp chipotle paste
1 small garlic clove, crushed
zest of ½ lime

TO SERVE
burger buns
1 large avocado
juice of ½ lime
lettuce leaves
sliced tomato
sliced red onions, soaked in salty water for 30 minutes, then drained
coriander sprigs

There's a great mix of textures and flavours here, resulting in a perfect veggie burger. I like to cook these on the barbecue, but as you roast the aubergine and onion first you get some lovely smokiness anyway.

1. Preheat the oven to 200°C/Fan 180°C/Gas 6. Score a cross-hatch pattern over the cut sides of the aubergine, going almost through to the skin. Put the aubergine halves in a roasting tin with the red onion, then season with plenty of salt and sprinkle over the mixed herbs. Drizzle over the oil, making sure it coats the aubergine and the onion. Roast in the oven for about 40 minutes, adding the garlic after 25 minutes. The onion wedges should be tender and slightly crisp around the edges and the aubergine halves should be softened.

2. Remove the aubergine and onion wedges from the oven. Roughly chop them and place them in a colander to drain. There will probably be quite a bit of liquid, so squeeze gently to get rid of any excess. Squeeze the flesh out of the garlic and discard the papery skins.

3. Put the beans in a bowl and mash them roughly so you get a good mix of whole and crushed beans. Add the breadcrumbs, cumin and sesame seeds, tomato purée and chipotle paste together with the aubergine, onion and garlic, then season with plenty of salt and pepper and mix thoroughly. Leave the mixture to chill in the fridge for at least an hour or, if you are in a hurry, in the freezer for 15 minutes.

4. Shape the mixture into 6 patties and brush them with olive oil. Mix the ingredients for the chipotle mayo together and season.

5. To barbecue the burgers, place them on a foil tray. Cook over a medium heat for 8–10 minutes, turning once, until a crust has developed on them and they are piping hot all the way through.

6. To oven bake, place the burgers on a baking tray and cook at 200°C/Fan 180°C/Gas 6 for about 15 minutes.

7. To fry or grill, heat a frying pan or griddle and add a little oil. Cook the burgers for 3–4 minutes or until a crust has developed, then flip and cook the other side.

8. To serve, lightly toast the burger buns. Mash the avocado flesh with the lime juice and plenty of salt. Smear the bottom halves of the buns with chipotle mayo and top with the burgers. Pile some of the avocado on top, followed by the lettuce, tomato, drained onion and coriander.

Baked sea bass with potatoes & lemon

SERVES 4

3 tbsp olive oil
1kg waxy or salad potatoes, cut into 5mm slices
2 leeks, finely sliced
100ml white wine
2 lemons (see method)
1 tsp fennel seeds
a few fresh oregano sprigs
a few rosemary sprigs
2 red chillies, finely sliced
2 sea bass, descaled and gutted
handful of samphire (optional)
sea salt and black pepper

This is a dead simple way of cooking whole fish – it's really a sort of fish one-pot and looks amazing. Adding diced lemon skin to the dish provides a nice bit of sourness, but as the lemon caramelises slightly it also adds sweetness to balance the heat from the chillies. Once the fish are cooked, the fillets should lift off the bone easily.

1. Preheat the oven to 200°C/Fan 180°C/Gas 6.

2. Put 2 tablespoons of the olive oil in a large roasting tin. Add the potatoes and leeks and turn them over in the oil. Season with salt and lots of black pepper, then pour over the wine with 100ml of water.

3. Juice both the lemons and zest one of them, then set the juice and zest aside. Take one of the juiced, unzested halves and finely chop it. Add it to the roasting tin along with half the fennel seeds, herbs and sliced chillies.

4. Roast the vegetables in the oven for 35 minutes, turning regularly, until they are tender and most of the liquid has steamed off. The potatoes should be starting to crisp and brown around the edges.

5. Stuff the sea bass with the remaining fennel seeds, herbs and chillies. Cut slashes into the flesh of the sea bass. Mix the lemon zest with a teaspoon of crushed sea salt and the remaining olive oil. Brush this mixture over the sea bass, pushing it into the slashes. Pour most of the lemon juice over the potatoes, then place the fish on top. Drizzle over the rest of the lemon juice.

6. Roast in the oven for 10–15 minutes, until the sea bass is piping hot all the way through. If using the samphire, blanch it in boiling water, then scatter it over the fish. Serve with some greens or a salad.

Spicy seafood rice

SERVES 4

1 net of live mussels
200g shell-on prawns
2 tbsp groundnut or sunflower oil
450ml fish or seafood stock
200g tomatoes, roughly chopped (or use canned)
1 scotch bonnet, deseeded, or 2 or 3 red chillies
2 tbsp peanut or cashew butter (preferably smooth)
1 large red onion, finely diced
2 celery sticks, finely chopped
4 garlic cloves, finely chopped
1 tsp dried oregano
1 large thyme sprig
2 tbsp tomato purée
300g basmati rice, well rinsed
generous pinch of saffron, soaked in a little warm water
100g small piquanté peppers, halved
salt and black pepper

TO SERVE
a few sprigs of coriander, finely chopped
lime wedges
hot sauce

In my view, mussels really do have it all – they're nutritious, sustainable, cheap and best of all, really tasty. Partner them with some prawns and spicy rice for a one-pot wonder that will keep everyone happy.

1. First prepare the mussels. Pull off any beards and clean the mussels thoroughly, discarding any that don't immediately close when you tap them. Set aside until ready to use.

2. Peel and devein the prawns. Heat a teaspoon of the oil in a saucepan, add the prawns and sear them briefly on each side, then remove and set aside. Add the heads and shells and stir-fry until they have turned pink. Pour the stock into the pan and stir to deglaze the base of the pan. Heat to almost boiling point, then remove from the heat and leave to stand.

3. Put the tomatoes, scotch bonnet or chillies and the nut butter in a blender and blitz to a thick purée. Set aside.

4. Add the remaining oil to a sauté pan that has a lid. Add the onion and celery and sauté until soft and translucent. Add the garlic, oregano, thyme and tomato purée and stir for several minutes until the purée smells rich and starts to separate from the oil. Pour in the tomato, chilli and nut butter mixture. Continue to cook, stirring regularly, until it has reduced down to a thick paste.

5. Stir in the rice, then strain the stock and pour it into the pan over the rice. Add the saffron and stir gently, making sure the base of the pan is deglazed, then season with salt and pepper and drop in the piquanté peppers. Bring to the boil, then turn down the heat and cover the pan. Leave to simmer for about 15 minutes or until all the liquid has been absorbed by the rice and the rice is cooked.

6. Add the mussels to the pan, standing them upright. Put the lid on the pan and leave to steam over a very low heat until the mussels have opened. Discard any that don't open. Add the prawns to heat through.

7. Garnish with the coriander and serve with lime wedges and hot sauce.

BBQ chicken with ras-el-hanout

SERVES 4

8 pieces of chicken
(mixture of breast, thigh,
drumsticks), skin on and on
the bone
salt and black pepper

MARINADE
2 tbsp ras-el-hanout
2 tbsp honey
2 tbsp olive oil
1 tbsp red wine vinegar
2 tsp mixed dried herbs
juice and zest of 1 lemon
4 garlic cloves, crushed

SAUCE
3 garlic cloves, crushed
or grated
juice of ½ lemon
200ml Greek yoghurt

TO SERVE
lemon wedges

Please do give this a try. Ras-el-hanout is a wonderful mixture of loads of different spices and is available in supermarkets now. Dave and I have absolutely loved it ever since we first discovered it when travelling in Morocco some twenty years ago. This chicken dish is epic when cooked on the barbecue but still tastes great done in the oven.

1. To make the marinade, mix all the ingredients together with plenty of salt, making sure the honey dissolves.

2. Cut slashes in the chicken, going through the skin and into the flesh. Season the chicken pieces with salt, then put them in a large bowl. Pour over the marinade and rub it into the chicken, then leave in the fridge for several hours, or overnight.

3. Remove the chicken from the fridge an hour before you want to start cooking it. Scrape off any excess marinade and set it aside. Pat the chicken dry.

4. If barbecuing the chicken, place it over an indirect heat and cover with the barbecue hood or lid. Cook the chicken for 35–40 minutes, turning it regularly, until cooked through. Then transfer to the direct heat, uncovered, for a further 10 minutes to crisp up the skin. At this point, baste with any remaining marinade. Keep a close eye on the chicken while it is over the direct heat as it can burn very quickly.

5. To cook the chicken in the oven, preheat the oven to 200°C/Fan 180°C/ Gas 6. Arrange the chicken on a rack over a roasting tin, then roast for 45 minutes or so, turning at least a couple of times, until it's cooked through and the skin is crisp and slightly charred. If you have a probe, the internal temperature should be 72°C.

6. To make the sauce, stir the garlic and lemon juice into the yoghurt and season with plenty of salt and pepper. Serve the chicken with lemon wedges and the yoghurt sauce.

Chicken enchiladas

SERVES 4

ENCHILADA SAUCE
1 tbsp olive oil
1 small onion, very finely
    chopped
4 garlic cloves, finely chopped
1½ tbsp spice mix (see p.267)
    or a shop-bought taco spice
    mix
2 tbsp tomato purée
2 tsp chipotle paste or hot
    sauce
800g canned tomatoes or
    passata
1 bay leaf
salt and black pepper

CHICKEN
1 tbsp olive oil
2 red onions, sliced
2 red peppers, sliced
1 tsp cumin seeds
about 400g skinless,
    boneless chicken breast or
    thigh meat, cut into strips
2 garlic cloves, finely chopped
2 tbsp finely chopped
    coriander stems

TO ASSEMBLE
8 tortillas, lightly toasted
250g soured cream (optional)
coriander leaves
150g Cheddar, grated
pickled jalapeños (optional)

TO SERVE
lime wedges
soured cream

Even just the word 'enchilada' puts a smile on my face. It makes me think of evenings with a few mates enjoying this fun Mexican dish and a couple of beers. Nothing better.

1. First make the enchilada sauce. Heat the olive oil in a saucepan and add the onion. Sauté until soft and translucent, then stir in the garlic. Cook for another couple of minutes, then stir in the spice mix, followed by the tomato purée and the chipotle paste or hot sauce. Stir until the tomato purée starts to smell intensely savoury, then stir in the tomatoes with 100ml of water. Drop in the bay leaf.

2. Stir thoroughly to combine, then season with salt and pepper. Leave the sauce to simmer, uncovered, over a low heat for about half an hour until it has reduced. Remove the bay leaf, then blitz the sauce with a stick or jug blender.

3. To make the chicken filling, heat the olive oil in a large frying pan. Add the onions and peppers and cook over a high heat until they're starting to soften and take on some colour. Stir in the cumin seeds, then add the chicken. Continue to fry until the chicken is just cooked through, then add the garlic and coriander stems. Cook for another couple of minutes, then add a ladleful of the enchilada sauce to coat the chicken and the vegetables. Preheat the oven to 200°C/Fan 180°C/Gas 6.

4. To assemble, toast the tortillas in a dry frying pan (this keeps them from going soggy). Divide the chicken mixture between the tortillas and roll them up. Spread a couple of ladlefuls of enchilada sauce over the base of a large ovenproof dish, then arrange the filled tortillas over the top, with the join-side down.

5. Ladle over more of the sauce but don't cover the tortillas completely – leave the edges uncovered so they crisp up. Dot over spoonfuls of the soured cream, if using, then sprinkle with coriander, Cheddar and pickled jalapeños, if using.

6. Bake in the preheated oven for 20–25 minutes until the cheese has melted and the sauce is bubbling. Serve with lime wedges and dollops of extra soured cream.

Duck à l'orange

SERVES 4

4 duck legs
4 tsp rum or brandy
1 Seville orange, thickly sliced
1 onion, thickly sliced
a few thyme sprigs
a few allspice berries, lightly
    crushed
4 bay leaves
8 garlic cloves, lightly
    squashed (unpeeled)
salt and white or black pepper

SAUCE
3 Seville oranges
50g granulated sugar
1 tbsp cider vinegar
3 shallots, very finely chopped
2 garlic cloves, very finely
    chopped
250ml well-flavoured chicken
    or duck stock

When duck à l'orange is cooked properly it is a gastronomic triumph and your friends will be well impressed. For best results, make this when Seville oranges are in season. You could put ordinary oranges under the roasting duck but the zest really should be from Sevilles – or use a couple of spoonfuls of Seville orange marmalade instead.

1. Preheat the oven to 200°C/Fan 180°C/Gas 6. Take the duck legs and pierce the skin all over with a fork, skewer or knife tip. Put the duck legs in a colander, place them in the sink and pour over 2 kettlefuls of freshly boiled water. Pat the duck dry, then rub the rum or brandy over the skin of each duck leg. Sprinkle with plenty of sea salt and freshly ground pepper – white if you have it, black if not.

2. Arrange the orange and onion slices over the base of a roasting tin. Top with the thyme, allspice berries, bay leaves and garlic. Place the duck legs on top, skin-side up, and add 200ml of freshly boiled water to the tin. Roast in the oven for 40–45 minutes, until the duck legs are cooked through and the skin is crisp. Remove the duck legs from the oven and leave them to rest. Strain off any pan juices and leave them to settle – the fat will rise to the top and can be skimmed off and saved.

3. Meanwhile, make the sauce. Pare off the zest from the oranges (a peeler makes quick work of this), then trim off any excess pith. Cut the zest into matchstick strips, put them in a pan and cover with freshly boiled water. Bring back to the boil and cook the zest for 3 minutes to blanch – this will remove any excess bitterness. Drain and set aside. Juice the oranges.

4. Put the sugar in a pan and give it a shake so it is in an even layer. Pour over 50ml of water – the mixture will have the texture of wet sand. Heat until the sugar has dissolved, then add the zest. Continue to cook for several minutes until the mixture looks syrupy, then remove the zest with a slotted spoon and set aside. Add the vinegar to the pan, then turn up the heat and boil until the sugar caramelises – it should be a rich golden colour. Watch it like a hawk at this point and don't let it go too dark.

5. Reduce the heat, then add the shallots, garlic and all the orange juice. Be very careful when you add the juice because the caramel will probably spit and seize up (turn solid again) when the liquid is added. When the spitting has stopped, stir until the caramel has dissolved again, then add the stock and simmer until the sauce is syrupy. It can be made ahead to this point. Add the roasting tin juices to the sauce and reheat until piping hot. Stir the zest back in just before serving with the duck legs.

Chicken dhansak curry

SERVES 4

8 chicken thighs, skin on and
    on the bone
juice of 1 lemon
2 tbsp olive or coconut oil
2 large onions, finely sliced
15g root ginger, grated
6 garlic cloves, crushed or
    grated
2 tbsp dhansak curry powder
    (shop-bought or see p.267)
2 tbsp tomato purée
2 tbsp tamarind paste
150g split red lentils, well
    rinsed
500ml chicken stock
2 bay leaves
salt and black pepper

TO SERVE
basmati rice
green chillies
leaves from a few coriander
    sprigs
100ml plain yoghurt

Dave and I first met in 1992 over a few pints of beer, four poppadoms and a chicken dhansak in the Egypt Cottage pub next to the old Tyne Tees TV studios. What a way to start a lifelong friendship! This has always been one of our very favourite curries.

1. Season the chicken with plenty of salt, then pour over the lemon juice and leave to stand for half an hour.

2. Heat the olive or coconut oil in a large flameproof casserole dish or a sauté pan. Add the chicken thighs, skin-side down, and sear until they're lightly browned. Flip them over and cook for another few minutes, then remove them from the pan.

3. Add the onions and cook over a medium heat until lightly coloured and starting to soften Add the ginger, garlic and curry powder and cook for a couple of minutes, then stir in the tomato purée and tamarind paste.

4. Put the chicken back in the pan, turning it over in the spices, then sprinkle in the lentils. Pour over the stock and tuck in the bay leaves. Season with salt.

5. Bring to the boil, stirring to make sure nothing is sticking to the base of the pan, then cover and turn down the heat to a simmer. Cook for about 45 minutes, until the chicken is tender and the lentils have softened and are close to collapsing. Check regularly to make sure nothing is catching and add a splash more water if necessary.

6. Sprinkle with a little more curry powder and serve with some rice, green chillies and coriander and some yoghurt on the side.

Roast chicken with preserved lemon

SERVES 4

1 chicken
25g butter, softened
1 small preserved lemon,
    deseeded and finely
    chopped
1 garlic clove, finely chopped
2 onions, thickly sliced
1 large thyme sprig
juice of 1 lemon
100ml white wine
salt and black pepper

STUFFING

1 tbsp olive oil
1 small onion, finely chopped
2 garlic cloves, finely chopped
2 tbsp pistachios, roughly
    chopped
1 small preserved lemon,
    deseeded and very finely
    chopped
zest of 1 lemon
½ tsp dried mint
½ tsp ground allspice
1 tsp dried oregano
2 tbsp finely chopped parsley
75g breadcrumbs
1 egg

I must have cooked this dish at least a hundred times – it's absolutely gorgeous. So if you fancy jazzing up your Sunday roast chicken with the wonderful flavours of preserved lemon, pistachios and dried mint, this one is definitely for you.

1. If you have time, the day before you plan on roasting your chicken, remove it from any packaging, place it on a plate and sprinkle with salt. Cover (wrapping in kitchen paper works best) and leave it in the fridge overnight. Remove from the fridge an hour before you want to cook it.

2. To make the stuffing, heat the olive oil in a frying pan and add the onion. Sauté until soft and translucent, then add the garlic and cook for a further minute. Transfer to a bowl and leave to cool. Add all the remaining ingredients and season generously, then stuff the mixture into the cavity of the chicken. Weigh the chicken now, so you can work out the roasting time. Preheat the oven to 220°C/Fan 200°C/Gas 7.

3. Mix the softened butter with the preserved lemon and garlic. Season with plenty of salt and pepper. Carefully work the skin away from the body of the chicken and spread half the butter under the skin over the breasts. Spread the rest on top of both breasts and legs.

4. Put the sliced onions into a roasting tin, add the thyme sprig and place the chicken on top. Sprinkle over the lemon juice, then pour the white wine into the roasting tin and add 100ml of water.

5. Put the chicken in the oven and roast it for 15 minutes. Turn the oven temperature down to 180°C/Fan 160°C/Gas 4 and roast for 15 minutes for every 500g.

6. Check the chicken is done. If you pierce the thickest part of the thigh, the skin should run clear. The legs should also feel loose when you wiggle them. If you have a probe thermometer, the thickest part of the thigh – and the temperature of the stuffing – should be 72°C.

7. When the chicken is cooked, transfer it to a warmed serving dish along with the roasted onions, cover it with foil and leave it to rest. Strain the roasting tin juices into a small pan. Deglaze the tin with a little water to scrape up any brown bits and add them to the roasting tin juices. Add any liquid that has pooled under the resting chicken and reheat to piping hot. Serve the chicken with the pan juices.

Chinese duck pancakes

SERVES 4

2 duck breasts
2 duck legs
1 tsp Chinese five spice
 powder
½ tsp chilli powder
1 tsp honey
1 tbsp light soy sauce
20 Chinese pancakes (see
 p.270 or shop-bought)
salt

PLUM SAUCE

400g plums (about 4 large or
 6 medium), stones removed
50g light brown soft sugar
10g root ginger, finely
 chopped or grated
1 garlic clove
2 star anise
½ tsp Chinese five spice
 powder
2 tbsp dark soy sauce
2 tsp rice vinegar

TO SERVE

1 cucumber, cut into batons
1 bunch of spring onions,
 halved and shredded

This is a familiar takeaway and restaurant dish that Dave and I have always enjoyed, but when you make it at home, using our simplified way of preparing the duck, there's something very special about it. You can buy the Chinese pancakes, but we've put a recipe in the back if you feel like making your own. The plum sauce is really good or you could just use hoisin sauce.

1. Start the duck several hours – or preferably the day before – you want to roast it. Using a sharp knife, score a cross-hatch pattern through the skin and fat of the breasts, almost through to the flesh. Use a skewer to pierce holes in the skin of the duck legs.

2. Put the pieces of duck in a colander, place it in the sink and pour over 2 kettlefuls of freshly boiled water. Pat the duck dry, then place it all on a rack and sprinkle with salt. Mix the Chinese five spice with the chilli powder, honey and soy sauce and brush this all over the duck. Leave it in the fridge for several hours or overnight.

3. To make the plum sauce, put all the ingredients into a saucepan. Heat gently, stirring until the plums start releasing liquid and the sugar has dissolved. When the plums have collapsed down completely, bring the sauce to the boil, then turn the heat down and simmer for 5 minutes. Remove from the heat and leave to stand for 5 minutes, then push the sauce through a sieve. Store it in the fridge until you need it.

4. To cook the duck, preheat the oven to 200°C/Fan 180°C/Gas 6. Put the duck pieces, skin-side down, in a large frying pan – an ovenproof one is best. Gradually heat the pan to a medium-low heat, then cook the duck on the hob for 12–15 minutes – this will render out plenty of fat without browning the skin too much.

5. Transfer the duck to the oven – either in the ovenproof frying pan or put it in a roasting tin – and continue to cook, skin-side down, for another 20 minutes. Reduce the oven temperature to 150°C/Fan 130°C/Gas 2. Flip the duck so it is skin-side up and cook for another 45–50 minutes until it is completely cooked through and the leg meat falls off the bone easily. Transfer the duck to a chopping board and shred the meat with 2 forks.

6. While the duck is cooking, prepare the pancakes or, if using shop-bought pancakes, warm them through. Serve the duck with the pancakes, plum sauce, cucumber and spring onions.

Coronation chicken pancakes

SERVES 4

PANCAKES

1 small bunch of coriander,
   roughly chopped
100g plain flour
1 tsp salt
1 egg
275ml whole milk
½ tsp mustard seeds
½ tsp nigella seeds
coconut oil or butter, for
   frying

FILLING

zest and juice of 1 lime
1 garlic clove, crushed or
   grated
1 tsp curry powder
1 tsp hot sauce or ½ tsp hot
   chilli flakes
2 tbsp olive oil
300g cooked chicken (breast
   or thigh, or a combination)
1 mango, peeled and diced
4 spring onions, finely
   chopped
1 small bunch of coriander,
   finely chopped
300g baby leaf spinach
2 tbsp mango chutney
1 red or green chilli, finely
   chopped
salt and black pepper

RAITA

½ cucumber, deseeded and
   grated
250g yoghurt
1 tsp dried mint

A proper crowd pleaser, this takes coronation chicken to another level. It's best served with the spinach and pancakes still slightly warm rather than hot, and the yoghurt refreshingly cool.

1. First make the pancakes. Put the roughly chopped coriander in a small food processor with 25ml of water and blitz until well broken down but not completely smooth.

2. Put the flour into a bowl with the salt. Add the egg and work it into the flour until you have a thick paste, then gradually beat in all of the milk to make a smooth batter. Add the mustard and nigella seeds and the coriander mixture and leave to stand for half an hour.

3. Heat a crepe pan – one that's about 20cm in diameter is ideal. When it's hot, add a small knob of coconut oil or butter. When it has melted, add a ladleful of the batter, swirling it around so it covers the entire base of the pan. Leave the pancake to set. When you can see it is browning around the edges and can easily be peeled off the pan, flip and continue to cook. Transfer the pancake to a plate and keep it warm. Repeat until you have made 8 pancakes.

4. For the filling, put the lime zest and juice, garlic, curry powder, hot sauce or chilli flakes and olive oil in a large bowl. Add a generous pinch of salt and some black pepper and then whisk. Add the chicken, mango chutney, spring onions and half the coriander and toss to combine.

5. For the raita, put the cucumber in a colander or sieve and set it over a bowl. Sprinkle with salt and mix, then leave to stand for half an hour. Gently squeeze out the moisture, then mix with the yoghurt and mint.

6. Put the spinach into a wide sauté pan (no water necessary) and sprinkle with a little salt. Wilt it over a high heat, stirring until it has collapsed but is still recognisably spinach.

7. To assemble, spread each pancake with a little mango chutney. Arrange some spinach over one half, then top with the chicken, followed by some raita. Continue until you have assembled all the pancakes, then garnish with chopped chilli and the rest of the coriander.

Thai pot-roast chicken

SERVES 4–6

1 chicken
1 Thai basil sprig
a few coriander sprigs
1 lemongrass stalk, bruised
2 lime leaves, bruised
a pared piece of lime zest
3 garlic cloves, bruised
salt

FOR THE POT
2 tbsp olive oil
8 banana shallots, peeled
4 tbsp Thai red curry paste
    (shop-bought or see p.266)
200ml coconut milk
200ml chicken stock
1–2 tbsp fish sauce
2 lime leaves, shredded
juice of ½ lime

TO SERVE
roughly torn coriander leaves
roughly torn Thai basil
3 spring onions, halved and
    shredded
2 red chillies, finely sliced
lime wedges

My son Alex invented this dish and rang me the minute he'd tasted it. He said, 'Dad, you've got to try my special pot-roast.' So I did and that's why it's in this book. It's fabulous and a new family favourite for us.

1. Preheat the oven to 200°C/Fan 180°C/Gas 6.

2. Sprinkle the inside and outside of the chicken with salt. Stuff with the herbs, lemongrass, lime leaves, lime zest and the garlic.

3. Heat half the oil in a large flameproof casserole dish. Add the shallots and sear them until lightly browned all over, then remove and set aside.

4. Add the rest of the olive oil to the dish with the red curry paste. Stir for a few minutes until the paste has darkened a little and the aroma has strengthened, then add the chicken, breast-side down, and leave to sear for a couple of minutes.

5. Remove the chicken and set it aside, then add the coconut milk, stock, a tablespoon of the fish sauce, the lime leaves and lime juice to the dish. Stir to make sure the base of the casserole dish is deglazed, then place the chicken back in the dish, this time breast-side up.

6. Cover the casserole dish and place it in the oven. Leave for 40 minutes, or so, until the chicken is almost cooked through, then remove the lid. Add the seared shallots to the dish, then put it back in the oven for about 20–25 minutes, until the sauce has reduced a little and both the shallots and chicken are tender. You can check the chicken for doneness by inserting a probe thermometer into the thickest part of the thigh – it should reach 72°C. Alternatively, check that the juices run clear when you insert a skewer and that the legs feel loose.

7. Remove the casserole dish from the oven. Taste the sauce and add more fish sauce if necessary. Leave the chicken to rest for 10 minutes, then serve garnished with the herbs, spring onions, chillies and the lime wedges on the side. This is good with rice or perhaps some noodles with some fresh root ginger stirred through them.

Proper lasagne

SERVES 6

RAGÙ
350g minced beef
150g minced pork
2 tbsp olive oil
1 onion, very finely chopped
1 carrot, very finely chopped
2 celery sticks, very finely
    chopped
50g chicken livers (optional),
    finely chopped
3 garlic cloves, finely chopped
1 tsp dried oregano
1 bay leaf
1 thyme sprig
100ml whole milk
250ml red wine
1 tbsp tomato purée
400g crushed tomatoes or
    passata
250ml beef or chicken stock

TO ASSEMBLE
1 quantity of béchamel sauce
    (see p.261)
12 lasagne sheets
100g 'nduja
nutmeg, for grating
50g Parmesan, grated
basil leaves
2 balls of mozzarella, very
    thinly sliced

Always a winner, this is a proper hearty lasagne with a little kick of 'nduja in the meaty sauce. And while you're at it, make the work count and cook double the quantity of ragù. Stash what you don't use in the freezer for another time.

1. Heat a large frying pan. Add the beef and pork, squashing it all flat into the base of the pan. Leave for 2–3 minutes until a crust has formed, then break the meat up and turn it over to brown the other side. When the meat is well browned, remove the pan from the heat.

2. Heat the oil in a large saucepan. Add the onion, carrot and celery, then sauté gently until the onion is starting to soften and turn translucent. Turn up the heat a little and add the chicken livers, if using. When they are browned, stir in the garlic and the herbs and continue to cook for another minute.

3. Add the browned meat to the saucepan. Season with plenty of salt and pepper, then pour in the milk. Stir so the meat is well coated, then turn down the heat and cook until the milk has evaporated off.

4. Turn up the heat again and pour in the wine. Leave it to bubble until it has reduced by half, then stir in the tomato purée, followed by the tomatoes or passata and the stock. Stir thoroughly to make sure the base of the pan is deglazed. Bring to the boil, then turn down the heat again and leave to simmer, covered, for about an hour or longer if you have time. Remove the lid and continue to simmer until the sauce has reduced a little – it should be thick, rather than pourable.

5. Make the béchamel according to the recipe on page 261. Preheat the oven to 200°C/Fan 180°C/Gas 6.

6. To assemble the lasagne, spread a quarter of the ragù over the base of a 30 x 20cm ovenproof dish. Ladle a fifth of the béchamel over the ragù then arrange 3 of the lasagne sheets over the top. Repeat with more ragù and béchamel, but this time dot spoonfuls of the 'nduja over the top, along with a rasp of nutmeg, a little grated Parmesan and some torn basil leaves. Top with more lasagne sheets and repeat twice more until you have used up all the ragù. Pour the remaining béchamel over the top layer of lasagne, then arrange the mozzarella on top along with a final sprinkling of Parmesan.

7. Bake in the oven for 40–45 minutes until the pasta sheets have softened and everything is piping hot. Remove from the oven and leave to stand for at least 10 minutes before serving.

Ginger beer glazed ham

SERVES 8

1 x 2kg rolled ham (gammon) joint (smoked or unsmoked)

500ml alcoholic ginger beer (such as Crabbies)

750ml–1 litre non-alcoholic ginger beer (such as Fentimans)

1 onion, quartered

2 bay leaves

4 garlic cloves, lightly crushed

1 tsp black peppercorns, lightly crushed

1 tsp allspice berries, lightly crushed

GLAZE

1 tbsp cloves

1 tbsp tamarind paste

50g dark brown soft sugar

2 tsp ground ginger

TO SERVE

grilled pineapple

Simple but special, this is a real favourite, as the ginger beer and the ginger glaze really bring out the best in the flavour of the ham. The cooking liquor tastes delicious and makes an excellent base for soup, especially a bean one. Just ask your butcher whether the ham needs to be soaked overnight or not.

1. Put the ham joint into a saucepan or a flameproof casserole dish just large enough to hold it comfortably, then pour over the ginger beers. Top up with a little water if the ham isn't completely covered. Add the aromatics and bring to the boil, then turn the heat down and simmer, partially covered, until the ham is cooked through. For a 2kg ham this will take about an hour and 50 minutes to 2 hours. If you have a probe thermometer the internal temperature should read at least 68°C. If not, pierce with a skewer – if, when you withdraw the skewer, it's almost too hot to touch for more than a second, the ham will be done.

2. Remove the ham from the cooking liquor and put it on a board to drain. Set the liquor aside. Cut off any string and trim away some of the fat, leaving a rim about a couple of millimetres thick. Score a diamond pattern through the fat and stud the corners with cloves.

3. Put the tamarind paste, sugar and ground ginger into a small saucepan. Add 2 tablespoons of the cooking liquor and stir over a low heat until the sugar has dissolved. Simmer until you have a thick syrup, then rub this over the ham.

4. Preheat the oven to 200°C/Fan 180°C/Gas 6. Put the ham in a roasting tin and cook for 15–20 minutes until the glaze has browned. Lovely served with some slices of grilled pineapple.

Coffee & chilli brisket

SERVES 4-6

1kg beef brisket, preferably in
    one piece
2 onions, cut into wedges
1 head of garlic, broken into
    cloves, unpeeled
300ml beef stock or water

RUB

3 tbsp ground coffee
1½ tbsp cardamom pods,
    seeds only
1 tsp cumin seeds
1 tsp black peppercorns
1 tbsp chilli powder
1 tsp garlic powder
1 tsp cinnamon
1 tbsp light brown soft sugar
1 tsp sea salt
1 tbsp red wine vinegar
3 tbsp olive oil

TO SERVE
cornbread (see p.264)

A funky, flavoursome take on the good old brisket, this has a bit of a South Asian vibe with the cardamom which works so well with the coffee. The meat has to marinate and needs quite a long time in the oven but there's very little hands-on work for such a rewarding dish.

1. To make the rub, put the coffee, cardamom seeds, cumin seeds and peppercorns into a spice grinder and blitz to a powder. Mix with the remaining spices, the sugar and salt, then stir in the red wine vinegar and oil. Rub this mixture all over the brisket, then leave it in the fridge to marinate for several hours, or overnight if possible.

2. Remove the beef from the fridge an hour before you want to start cooking it, so it can come up to room temperature. Preheat the oven to 200°C/Fan 180°C/Gas 6.

3. Scatter the onions over the base of a roasting tin or a flameproof casserole dish, then sprinkle over the garlic cloves and place the beef on top. Pour the stock or water around the beef. If using a roasting tin, cover it tightly with foil. If using a casserole dish, put the lid on.

4. Place in the preheated oven and cook for about an hour and a half. Remove from the oven and turn the beef over and continue to cook for another hour and a half. At this point the beef should be cooked to a slightly firm, sliceable consistency. If you want the meat much softer so it can be pulled apart, you could cook it for another hour.

5. When the beef is cooked to your liking, remove the foil or lid and cook uncovered for a further 20 minutes. Remove the beef, cover it with foil and leave it to rest.

6. Transfer the cooking liquor and onions to a saucepan. Squeeze the flesh out of the garlic cloves and add it to the liquor, then reduce to a syrupy gravy to serve as a sauce with the beef. Freshly baked cornbread makes a great side dish.

Caribbean BBQ lamb ribs

SERVES 4

1kg lamb ribs

MARINADE

1–2 scotch bonnet chillies,
    (deseeding optional)
4 spring onions, roughly
    chopped
6 garlic cloves, peeled
5g root ginger, roughly
    chopped
leaves from a large thyme
    sprig
1 tbsp cider vinegar
1 tbsp dark brown soft sugar
2 tsp ground allspice
1 tsp ground cumin
½ tsp ground cinnamon
a few gratings of nutmeg
1 tbsp olive oil
juice and zest of 1 lime
2 tbsp crumbled bay leaves
salt and black pepper

TO FINISH

2 tbsp beer (any kind), plus
    extra to spray if needed
2 spring onions, finely
    chopped

Dave and I have always loved jerk chicken and we've tweaked our jerk marinade to suit the flavour of lamb. The reason the ribs are twice cooked is that they have quite a bit of fat and simmering helps render some of this out, making the ribs crisper. You might like to strain off the liquor after cooking the ribs. Once the fat has settled on top, the liquid underneath makes a good, spicy, meaty stock for a Caribbean curry or a bean soup. Waste not, want not, I always say.

1. Put all the marinade ingredients, except the bay leaves, into a food processor with plenty of salt and pepper. Blitz until well broken down, then add the bay leaves. Season the lamb ribs with more salt and pour the marinade over them. Mix thoroughly so the ribs are well coated, then set aside to marinate for at least an hour or leave in the fridge overnight.

2. When you're ready to cook the ribs, scrape off any excess marinade and set it aside. Put the ribs in a saucepan or a flameproof casserole dish and cover them with water. Slowly bring them to the boil, then turn the heat down and simmer for 25–30 minutes until the lamb ribs are just tender.

3. Remove the lamb ribs from the cooking liquor. If oven baking the ribs, preheat the oven to 220°C/Fan 200°C/Gas 7 and arrange them on a rack. Mix the reserved marinade with the 2 tablespoons of beer. Brush the marinade liberally over the ribs, then bake them for about 30 minutes, basting with the marinade and turning regularly, until they are crisp and well browned.

4. If barbecuing, cook the ribs over indirect heat for 10–15 minutes, then over the direct heat for another 10, until they are smoky and nicely charred. Baste the ribs regularly and spray them with a little beer if they are browning too quickly. Serve sprinkled with spring onions.

Slow-cooked lamb shoulder

1 shoulder of lamb, on the
    bone
2 onions, thickly sliced
3 bay leaves
2 thyme sprigs
salt and black pepper

MARINADE
1 tbsp Baharat spice
zest and juice of 1 lemon
2 tbsp pomegranate molasses
2 garlic cloves, crushed
25g yoghurt
1 tbsp olive oil

VEGETABLES
1 large red onion, very finely
    sliced
juice of 1 lime
½ red cabbage, shredded
2 roasted red peppers, finely
    sliced
2 pickled chillies, finely sliced
1 tbsp red wine vinegar
1 tsp sumac
seeds from ½ pomegranate

GARLIC SAUCE
200g yoghurt
1 tbsp olive oil
juice of ½ lemon
1 garlic clove, crushed
large pinch of sugar

TO SERVE
flatbreads (shop-bought or
    see p.262)
chives and a few parsley,
    coriander, mint sprigs

I'm a big fan of slow-roast lamb, cooked in all these lovely spices and flavourings until the meat is so tender and soft it's falling off the bone. If you're cooking for a smaller number, you might want to go for a half shoulder, which will need about the same cooking time. Or do the whole thing and use the leftovers in our spicy lamb toasties on page 128.

1. Mix all the marinade ingredients together and season with plenty of salt and pepper. Score the skin of the lamb, then rub the marinade all over it. Leave for at least a couple of hours, but preferably overnight.

2. When you're ready to start cooking, preheat the oven to its highest setting. Arrange the onions over the base of a roasting tin and top with the bay leaves and thyme. Scrape off any excess marinade from the lamb and place the lamb on top of the onions. Cover the tin with foil.

3. Put the tin in the oven and right away turn the temperature down to 150°C/Fan 130°C/Gas 2. Cook until the meat is completely tender – the bone will become loose and should easily pull out. This will take at least 2½–3 hours.

4. Turn up the heat to 200°C/Fan 180°C/Gas 6, remove the foil and roast the lamb for another 25–30 minutes to crisp up the skin. Take the lamb out of the oven, then pull the meat apart with 2 forks, discarding any large pieces of fat.

5. While the lamb is roasting, prepare the vegetables. Put the red onion in a bowl. Sprinkle with half a teaspoon of salt and add the lime juice, then leave to stand for at least half an hour. Combine with the red cabbage, roast peppers and pickled chillies and drizzle over the red wine vinegar. Toss lightly, then sprinkle with the sumac and the pomegranate seeds.

6. Make the garlic sauce. Mix everything together with a generous amount of salt and pepper. Thin with 2–3 tablespoons of water.

7. Serve the lamb with the vegetables, garlic sauce, flatbreads and herbs, so everyone can help themselves.

TIP
To barbecue the lamb, wrap it in foil. Add some bay leaves and thyme to a foil tray on the coals as aromatics. Place the lamb over indirect heat and cook for several hours, covered with the lid or hood, until the meat is tender. Undo the foil parcel and cook the lamb over direct heat to crisp up the skin and get a little charring.

time for something sweet

66 As our careers in front of the camera developed, Dave, being the professional TV and film make-up artist that he was, always had a good eye for detail – particularly when it came to me. Now, as you all know, it could be said that my dress style is somewhat casual and my hair is just something that's on top of my head and gets very little attention. Dave, bless him, always took it upon himself to tidy me up a bit!99

Fruit & nut chocolate salami

100g raisins or chopped
    prunes
100ml rum or Marsala wine
    plus an optional extra tbsp
75g dark chocolate
175g cold butter, diced
4 egg yolks
150g caster sugar
75g cocoa powder
200g hazelnuts or almonds,
    lightly toasted and broken
    up
100g dark glacé cherries,
    halved
200g biscuits (shortbread or
    similar), broken into 1cm
    pieces
3 tbsp icing sugar
½ tsp ground cinnamon
    (optional)

Dave's family have always loved this sweet treat which has its roots in a traditional Romanian recipe. We've added some dried fruit, glacé cherries, nuts and a tot of alcohol to make it even more delicious. At Christmas, you could make smaller logs and wrap them up like Christmas crackers to give as presents.

1. Put the raisins or prunes into a small saucepan and cover them with the 100ml of rum or Marsala. Bring to the boil, then remove from the heat and leave to stand until the liquid has been absorbed by the fruit.

2. Put the chocolate in a heatproof bowl and set the bowl over a pan of simmering water. Let the chocolate to melt, then remove the bowl from the heat. Leave to cool for 5 minutes then add the butter – the butter will melt and help cool down the chocolate at the same time. Whisk them together until smooth. Beat in the tablespoon of rum or Marsala, if using.

3. Put the egg yolks into a large bowl with the sugar and beat to a smooth paste. Pour in the chocolate and butter, add the cocoa powder and mix together until you have a thick chocolate paste. Add the dried fruit, nuts cherries and biscuits, then stir thoroughly again. The mixture will be quite soft at this stage, but it will firm up quickly in the fridge.

4. Take 2 pieces of baking parchment and dust the icing sugar and the cinnamon, if using, over them. Divide the mixture in half and with wet hands, shape it into 2 log shapes, each about 20cm long and 5–6cm in diameter. Place each log on a piece of baking parchment and roll them up as tightly as you can, then wrap again in foil.

5. Leave to set and chill in the fridge for several hours, preferably overnight. Serve sliced into rounds.

Stollen bites

MAKES ABOUT 30

100g raisins, sultanas or
  currants, roughly chopped
  if large
50ml hot tea
2 tbsp rum
75g candied peel, finely diced
50g glacé cherries, rinsed of
  syrup and chopped
zest of 1 orange
300g plain flour
100g ground almonds
½ tsp baking powder
½ tsp bicarbonate of soda
1 tsp ground cinnamon
¼ tsp each of allspice, cloves
  and cardamom
½ tsp salt
50g light brown soft sugar
125g butter, chilled and diced
1 egg
175g ricotta
125g marzipan

TO FINISH
100g butter
75g icing sugar, plus more for
  dusting

There's just something about these little mouthfuls of sweetness and spice – an all-time favourite in both our households in winter. Traditional stollen is made with a yeast dough but these are quicker and easier to make and still really delicious.

1. Put the raisins, sultanas or currants into a small saucepan and add the tea and rum. Bring to the boil, then turn the heat down to a simmer until most of the liquid has been absorbed. Remove from the heat and stir in the peel, cherries and orange zest. Leave to cool.

2. Preheat the oven to 180°C/Fan 160°C/Gas 4. Line a large baking tray with baking parchment.

3. Put the flour, ground almonds, raising agents, spices and salt into a large bowl, then stir in the sugar. Rub in the butter until the mixture resembles very fine breadcrumbs. Drain the fruit and add it along with the egg and ricotta to make a fairly firm but sticky dough.

4. Divide the dough into 30 pieces, each weighing about 40g. Cut the marzipan into 30 pieces. Gently soften and flatten a piece of marzipan with your hands and push it into the centre of a piece of dough. Shape the dough to make sure that the marzipan is fully encased and as much of the fruit is covered by dough as possible. Repeat to make the rest of the stollen bites.

5. Arrange them on the baking tray and bake in the preheated oven for 20–25 minutes until slightly raised and golden brown.

6. Meanwhile, melt the 100g of butter. As soon as you take the stollen bites out of the oven, brush them liberally with the butter, then dip them into icing sugar right away, so they are coated all over. Place them on a rack to cool. Dust with more icing sugar before serving.

Prune, coffee & walnut brownies

MAKES 9 SQUARES

125g pitted soft prunes
75ml brandy
150g butter
250g granulated sugar
75g cocoa powder
15g espresso powder
1 tsp vanilla extract
2 eggs
75g plain flour
½ tsp baking powder
large pinch of salt
100g dark chocolate (ideally
   one with a touch of coffee),
   roughly chopped into
   shards
100g walnuts or pecans,
   roughly chopped

Proper grown-up brownies, these are made with dark chocolate and a hint of coffee, with the surprise of a luscious prune in the middle of each piece. Little nuggets of pleasure. If you can bear to wait, leave the tin of brownies in the fridge overnight before cutting them into squares – it really improves the texture.

1. Preheat the oven to 180°C/Fan 160°C/Gas 4. Line a 20cm square brownie tin with baking parchment.

2. Put the prunes in a small pan and cover them with the brandy. Bring to the boil, then turn the heat down and simmer until the brandy has been absorbed. Set aside to cool.

3. Put the butter, sugar, cocoa and espresso powder into a heatproof bowl. Place the bowl over a pan of simmering water and leave until the butter has melted and the sugar has started to dissolve. Stir until everything is well combined – the mixture will probably be quite grainy initially. Remove the bowl from the heat and set aside to cool to room temperature.

4. Beat in the vanilla extract, followed by the eggs and whisk until the mixture is completely smooth. Mix the flour with the baking powder and salt, then add to the bowl. Lastly, fold in the chocolate and nuts.

5. Scrape the mixture into the tin, then press the prunes into it, spacing them evenly. Bake in the preheated oven for 20–25 minutes – a skewer should come out with a few crumbs attached, and the top should be set and shiny.

6. Leave to cool or place in the fridge overnight, then cut into squares.

Lemon curd & hazelnut slices

MAKES 15 RECTANGULAR SLICES OR 16 SQUARES

150g blanched hazelnuts
150g plain flour
75g icing sugar
175g butter, chilled and diced
1 egg yolk
500g lemon curd (see p.274 or
    shop-bought)

CRUMBLE TOPPING
50g plain flour
25g icing sugar
pinch of salt
50g butter, chilled and diced

You're going to love these – a shortbread base slathered with tangy lemon curd and a crumble topping. They really are mega good. You can, of course, buy lemon curd but these teatime slices are even better if you make your own curd from the recipe on page 274.

1. Line a 20cm square baking tin with baking parchment.

2. Toast the hazelnuts in a dry frying pan until their aroma intensifies, then remove the pan from the heat and leave the nuts to cool. Blitz them to the consistency of ground almonds in a food processor.

3. For the shortbread base, put 100g of the ground hazelnuts into a bowl with the plain flour and icing sugar. Rub in the butter, until the mixture resembles fine breadcrumbs, then stir in the egg yolk. You will end up with quite a sticky dough. Pile this into the prepared tin, spreading it as evenly as you can with a palette knife, then put it in the fridge for at least half an hour to firm up.

4. Meanwhile, make the crumble topping. Put the remaining 50g of ground hazelnuts in a bowl with the 50g of plain flour, 25g of icing sugar and a pinch of salt. Rub in the butter with your fingertips, then leave the mixture in the fridge to chill.

5. Preheat the oven to 170°C/Fan 150°C/Gas 3½. Prick the shortbread all over with a fork, then bake it for 20–25 minutes until set on top and starting to turn a very light golden colour around the edges. Remove from the oven and leave to cool.

6. Spread the lemon curd over the shortbread base, then sprinkle over the crumble mixture as evenly as you can. Place in the oven and bake, at 170°C/Fan 150°C/Gas 3½, for 25–30 minutes until the crumble topping is lightly coloured.

7. Remove from the oven and leave to cool completely before removing from the tin and cutting into slices.

Rum babas with grilled pineapple

MAKES 6

BABAS
225g strong white flour
5g fast-acting dried yeast
25g light brown soft sugar
½ tsp salt
75ml milk
2 eggs, beaten
75g butter, softened, plus
    extra for greasing

SUGAR SYRUP
500g caster sugar
200ml dark or spiced rum

GRILLED PINEAPPLE
6 pineapple rings
2 tbsp golden caster sugar

TO SERVE
clotted cream

Both our mams were keen on a rum baba, so this recipe is in their honour. We've added a touch of glamour in the form of the pineapple which sets the boozy babas off a treat.

1. A stand mixer does make it much easier to prepare the babas, but you can also use an electric hand mixer with a dough hook. Put the flour in a stand mixer or a bowl and stir in the yeast and sugar, then add the salt.

2. Heat the milk very gently until warmed through to blood temperature, then whisk in the eggs. Gradually work the milk and eggs into the flour mix – this will be very soft to start with, so it is easier to use a paddle attachment rather than a dough hook for this stage. When you have a very ragged, soft dough, start adding the 75g of butter a tablespoon at a time until fully incorporated.

3. Switch to the dough hook and knead until the dough is smooth and glossy – it will be quite sticky. Cover the bowl with a damp tea towel, then leave the dough to prove until not quite doubled in size.

4. Generously butter 6 dariole moulds or mini pudding basins. Divide the mixture between them – it will still be quite sticky, so having wet or buttered hands helps enormously. Leave the babas to rise again until each one has risen to a perfect dome.

5. Preheat the oven to 180°C/Fan 160°C/Gas 4. Put the babas on a baking tray and bake them in the oven for 20–25 minutes until they are a rich golden brown. Slide them out of the moulds and leave to cool. You can keep them in an airtight container until you are ready to use them – when slightly stale they absorb the syrup well.

6. To make the sugar syrup, put the sugar in a saucepan with 500ml of water and heat slowly until the sugar has dissolved. Bring to the boil for 5 minutes, then remove from the heat. Add the rum and leave to cool.

7. To soak the babas, put them in a dish which holds them quite snugly, then pour over the cooled syrup. Turn the babas regularly until they have absorbed most of the syrup – they will feel much heavier. Chill them until you are ready to serve.

8. To grill the pineapple, heat a griddle until hot. Sprinkle the pineapple slices with sugar and griddle for 2–3 minutes on each side until lightly charred and caramelised.

9. To serve, place a rum baba on top of a pineapple ring and spoon over any remaining syrup. Serve with clotted cream.

Blueberry & buttermilk streusel cake

MAKES 8–12 SLICES

175g plain flour, plus 1 tbsp
    for the blueberries
1 tsp baking powder
½ tsp bicarbonate of soda
pinch of salt
85g butter, at room
    temperature
100g caster sugar
50ml maple syrup
2 eggs
1 tsp vanilla extract
150ml buttermilk
250g blueberries

STREUSEL TOPPING
100g plain flour
50g cold butter, diced
75g demerara sugar
25g flaked almonds

This is a good-looking cake, so good looking you'd take it out for dinner! Buttermilk makes for a lovely moist sponge and with the blueberries and that crunchy streusel finish, you'll find this will vanish in moments.

1. Preheat the oven to 180°C/Fan 160°C/Gas 4. Line a 23cm round cake tin with baking parchment.

2. First make the streusel topping. Put the flour into a bowl with the butter. Rub the butter in – not quite as finely as you would do for pastry – then stir in 50g of the sugar and all the flaked almonds. Chill the mixture in the fridge until you are ready to bake the cake.

3. For the sponge, put the flour, baking powder and bicarb into a bowl with a generous pinch of salt. Put the butter and sugar into a separate bowl, or the bowl of a stand mixer, with the maple syrup and beat until well aerated and soft. Add the eggs, 1 at a time, along with a heaped tablespoon of the flour mixture, mixing lightly between each addition.

4. Whisk the vanilla extract into the buttermilk. Add the buttermilk to the sponge mixture in several batches, again with a heaped tablespoon of flour with each addition, until everything is incorporated.

5. Toss half the blueberries with the reserved tablespoon of flour. Scrape half the sponge mixture into the prepared tin, then sprinkle over the floured blueberries. Top with the remaining cake mixture – the odd blueberry might poke through, but that doesn't matter. Add the rest of the blueberries and push them down gently to help them sink into the sponge. Sprinkle over the streusel topping, followed by the remaining 25g of demerara sugar.

6. Bake in the oven for about 45 minutes until the cake is well risen and springy to the touch. Leave to cool in the tin for 10 minutes, then remove and place on a cooling rack. Nice served warm with cream or cold.

Baked Alaska

SERVES 8–10

CAKE BASE
150g plain flour
1 tsp baking powder
pinch of salt
125g butter, softened
125g caster sugar
zest of 2 limes
2 eggs

ICE CREAM
1 quantity of coconut ice
    cream (see p.275) or 750g
    shop-bought ice cream
1 mango, finely chopped
zest and juice of ½ lime
2 tbsp caster sugar

MERINGUE
4 egg whites
pinch of salt
175g caster sugar
1 tsp white vinegar
1 tsp cornflour

We couldn't have a book of our family favourites without including this show-stopper of a pud. It's one of those timeless recipes and if you're feeling a bit retro, get your flares on, play a seventies soundtrack and cook this. It's well worth it. Fine to use shop-bought ice cream if you're in a rush, but if you have time, try our coconut ice cream recipe on page 275. It's epic and it needs four egg yolks, which is handy as it leaves you with four egg whites for the Alaska meringue.

1. Take some slightly softened home-made or shop-bought ice cream. Make the ripple by puréeing the mango, lime zest and juice and caster sugar together. Carefully stir this through the ice cream, being careful not to mix so much that it disappears.

2. Line a 750ml–1 litre pudding bowl with a double layer of cling film, then pile the ice cream into it. Cover well and freeze, preferably overnight.

3. To make the cake, preheat the oven to 200°C/Fan 180°C/Gas 6 and line a 20cm round cake tin with baking parchment. Mix the flour with the baking powder and a generous pinch of salt. Beat the butter, sugar and lime zest together until soft and aerated, then beat in the eggs and flour. Scrape the mixture into the tin and smooth the top with a palette knife.

4. Bake the cake in the oven for about 25 minutes until lightly browned and firm to touch. Remove and leave to cool completely.

5. Before starting to make the meringue, remove the ice cream from the freezer. If it's absolutely solid, leave it at room temperature for at least 10 minutes. If it is softer, keep it in the fridge.

6. Put the egg whites in a bowl with a pinch of salt, then whisk to stiff peaks. Add a third of the sugar and beat to incorporate it, then repeat twice more until you have beaten in all the sugar and you have a thick, glossy meringue. Sprinkle over the vinegar and cornflour and whisk them in.

7. To assemble, preheat the oven to 240°C/Fan 220°C/Gas 9. Put the sponge in the centre of an ovenproof serving dish (a large ceramic flan dish works well), then unmould the ice cream, peeling off all the cling film, and place it on top of the sponge. Completely cover with the meringue, making sure that it is completely sealed – any hot air getting to the ice cream will start to melt it.

8. Put the dish in the oven and bake until the meringue has coloured – start checking after 3–4 minutes. The ice cream should be fine for 8–10 minutes. Remove from the oven and serve straight away.

Tiramisu

SERVES AT LEAST 6

75g dark chocolate, preferably
    at least 85% (see method)
250ml very strong coffee
2 tbsp rum
1 tbsp Marsala wine
18–24 sponge fingers
    (Savoirardi)
100g amaretti biscuits
500g mascarpone
3 eggs, separated
50g icing sugar

A great tiramisu is a true gastronomic wonder and this recipe is no exception. We like to use rum instead of the more traditional brandy, as we feel it goes so well with the coffee and chocolate, and we add amaretti as well as sponge fingers for a nice bit of crunch. A dessert with the wow factor and no oven needed.

1. Break up the chocolate and either cut it into very fine shards with a sharp knife, or put it into a food processor and blitz until fine. This is easier and much less messy than grating it. Set the chocolate aside.

2. Put the coffee in a bowl with the rum and Marsala. Dip the sponge fingers into the coffee mixture quite briefly – you don't want them to absorb so much liquid that they go soggy – then use them to line the base of a rectangular dish; 18 x 24cm is about right. Arrange the sponge fingers on their sides so you can squeeze more in and this also gives more height to the pudding.

3. Crumble up the amaretti and sprinkle them over the sponge fingers. Sprinkle some of the chocolate over the amaretti.

4. To make the custard, put the mascarpone in a bowl. Beat it with the egg yolks and sugar until smooth. Whisk the egg whites to the stiff peak stage, stopping short of them becoming very dry, then fold them into the mascarpone mixture. Make sure the egg whites are thoroughly incorporated, leaving no streaks. Spread this custard over the sponge fingers and amaretti, then sprinkle the rest of the chocolate on top.

5. Cover and leave to chill in the fridge for several hours before serving.

Green tea panna cottas with miso caramel

MAKES 6

PANNA COTTAS
oil, for greasing
600ml single cream
150ml milk
175g caster sugar
30g green tea leaves
large pinch of smoked tea
    leaves (optional)
1 small cinnamon stick
1 tsp cardamom pods
1 piece of pared lime zest
3 sheets of leaf gelatine

MISO CARAMEL
100g granulated sugar
150g double or whipping
    cream
1 tbsp white miso paste
3 tbsp sweet sherry

Dave and I were so pleased with this recipe, which features some quite unusual flavours with great success. We originally included mead in the caramel, having come up with the idea after visiting a mead-making business for one of our TV shows. We've tweaked the dish slightly for this book to include sherry instead of mead in the caramel, but if you have some mead lying around, go ahead and use it. Choose Lapsang or Russian Caravan for the smoked tea, if including.

1. Lightly oil 6 ramekins. Put the cream, milk, caster sugar, tea leaves (including the smoked tea leaves, if using), spices and lime zest into a saucepan. Slowly bring to the boil, stirring to dissolve the sugar, then remove the pan from the heat and set aside to cool for about 10 minutes.

2. Soak the leaf gelatine in cold water until soft and pliable. Wring out the gelatine and add it to the saucepan. Put the pan back on the hob and heat gently while stirring until the leaves of gelatine have dissolved, then remove the pan from the heat.

3. Strain the mixture into a jug through a fine sieve, then pour it into the ramekins. Leave them to cool to room temperature, then put them in the fridge. Leave the panna cottas to chill and set for at least 4 hours.

4. To make the caramel, put the sugar in a saucepan and add just enough water to give it the consistency of wet sand. Place the pan over a medium heat and leave the sugar to caramelise, giving the pan a shake every now and again and moving it around on the heat to ensure the caramel colours evenly.

5. When the caramel is a rich golden colour, remove the pan from the heat. Add the cream and whisk – move fast as the mixture can seize and bubble up if you don't whisk constantly. If the caramel does seize, set the pan over a low heat and stir until the sugar has dissolved again. Whisk in the miso paste and sherry.

6. Turn the panna cottas out and drizzle the miso caramel over the top.

Apricot tart

SERVES AT LEAST 6

1 ready-rolled sheet of
    all-butter puff pastry
12 apricots, quartered

CRÈME PÂTISSIÈRE
400ml whole milk
2 pieces of pared lemon zest
a few lemon verbena or lemon
    thyme leaves (optional)
65g caster sugar
5 egg yolks
20g plain flour
20g cornflour
pinch of salt

TO FINISH
2 tbsp apricot conserve
1 tsp brandy or apricot eau
    de vie (optional)
a few lemon verbena or lemon
    thyme leaves, to garnish

Please do cook this tart. It is to die for and the surprise of the crème pâtissière gets me proper excited. It's important to use apricots that aren't too ripe so they don't go mushy. Look for fruit that's firm and sweet, but not rock hard.

1. First make the crème pâtissière. Put the milk, lemon zest and the lemon verbena or lemon thyme leaves, if using, into a saucepan. Slowly heat until almost boiling, then remove the pan from the heat and leave the milk to cool and infuse.

2. Whisk together the sugar, egg yolks and flours with a pinch of salt. Reheat the milk until blood temperature, then pour it over the egg mixture from a height, whisking as you do so. Pour everything back into the saucepan.

3. Cook over a gentle heat, stirring constantly and making sure you get right to the edges, until the mixture starts to thicken. It will thicken quickly. At this point, beat or whisk vigorously to make sure there are no lumps and continue to cook for a couple of minutes. Tip the crème pâtissière into a container and put a layer of cling film over the top, touching the surface, to prevent a skin from forming. Chill in the fridge.

4. Preheat the oven to 200°C/Fan 180°C/Gas 4 and put a baking tray in to heat up. Unroll the pastry on to a rectangular baking tray or a 24–25cm flan tin. Trim any overhang as necessary, but don't trim the pastry too closely as you need to allow for shrinkage. Score a 1cm border all round the pastry, then leave it to chill in the freezer for 10–15 minutes.

5. Scrape the crème pâtissière on to the pastry and spread it out evenly with a palette knife. Arrange the apricot quarters over the top.

6. Put the tart tin on the preheated baking tray. Bake in the oven for about 35 minutes until the pastry is golden brown and lightly puffed up around the edges and the apricots are cooked.

7. Remove from the oven. Melt the apricot conserve in a small saucepan, add the alcohol if using, then brush the conserve over the apricots. Sprinkle the tart with lemon verbena or lemon thyme leaves and serve at room temperature.

Chocolate & peanut butter puddings

MAKES 6

melted butter, for brushing
175g dark chocolate, broken
    into pieces
150g butter
2 tbsp milk
½ tsp vanilla extract
pinch of salt
3 eggs and 3 egg yolks
85g caster sugar
50g plain flour
6 tsp peanut butter,
    preferably salted
3 tsp raspberry jam

TO SERVE
cream

We knew we couldn't have a sweet tooth section without a chocolate self-saucing pudding. Whenever Dave and I had dinner out together he would always go for chocolate pudding for dessert if it was on offer. These can be prepared ahead if you want. If the puddings are straight from the fridge, they will need 14 minutes in the oven; if they've been frozen, 15–16 minutes. Precise I know, but it works. You could put some cherries in kirsch inside instead of peanut butter and jam.

1. Brush 6 small pudding basins with melted butter.

2. Put the chocolate, butter and milk into a heatproof bowl and place over a saucepan of simmering water. Allow the chocolate and butter to melt, stirring regularly until smooth. Add the vanilla extract and a generous pinch of salt, then remove from the heat and leave to cool a little.

3. Put the eggs, egg yolks and caster sugar into a large bowl. Beat with electric beaters or in a stand mixer until the mixture is very aerated and mousse-like – you should be able trail a ribbon of the mixture across the top without it immediately vanishing.

4. Pour the chocolate mixture into the bowl around the sides of the egg mixture and sprinkle the flour over the top. Mix everything together gently – try to avoid knocking all the air out. The mixture will turn the colour of milk chocolate.

5. Divide half the mixture between the pudding basins – you should have about 2 tablespoons per basin. Put teaspoons of the peanut butter and half teaspoons of the jam in the centre of each basin, pushing it into the chocolate mixture a little so it isn't too raised, then top each basin with the remaining mixture.

6. Preheat the oven to 200°C/Fan 180°C/Gas 6. Place the puddings on a baking tray and bake in the oven for about 12 minutes, until they have risen and set. The puddings might be slightly crisp around the edges and when you gently press them, they will feel firm and springy. They may have dipped slightly in the middle – this is fine as long as they are well set.

7. Leave the puddings to stand for a minute before running a palette knife around the sides and turning them out. Serve with cream.

Praline fudge

MAKES ABOUT 25 PIECES

125g butter, diced
200ml condensed milk
100ml milk or evaporated
    milk
100ml maple syrup
350g caster sugar
½ tsp vanilla extract

PECANS
100g pecans
50g maple syrup
½ tsp vanilla extract
pinch of salt

Pop a little square of this into your mouth – it's a joy. We've given a couple of options here, depending on whether you like smooth fudge or grainy – I'm for grainy. By the way, any leftover condensed milk will keep for a while in the fridge if decanted into a jar, or you can freeze it.

1. First prepare the pecans. Put them in a dry frying pan and drizzle over the maple syrup and vanilla. Add a generous pinch of salt, then cook over a medium heat, stirring constantly. The maple syrup will caramelise around the pecans – it will go very sticky and clump together to start with, then will suddenly become drier. Do not leave the pan unattended, as the nuts can burn very quickly. Remove from the heat and leave to cool. Break the nuts up, trying not to get them too crumbly.

2. Line a 20 x 20cm baking tin with baking parchment.

3. Put all the fudge ingredients into a saucepan. Stir over a gentle heat to start with, until the sugar has dissolved and the butter has melted. Then turn up the heat and bring the mixture to the boil.

4. Continue to boil, stirring constantly, until the mixture reaches the soft-ball stage. To test, either check with a thermometer – the mixture should reach 112–116°C – or drop small amounts into a bowl of cold water; the mixture should immediately set and form a soft ball. Start testing after 10 minutes but it can take up to 20 minutes for the fudge to be ready.

5. At this point you have two choices: you can either pour the fudge straight into your prepared tin – this will give you a smooth fudge. Or you can beat until the mixture has thickened and starts going grainy – this will give you a sandier texture which is more like a traditional Scottish tablet. If you decide to make the grainier fudge, it is best to beat with electric beaters as it is quite hard work.

6. When the fudge is to your liking, pour or scrape it into the prepared tin. Sprinkle over the pecans, then press them down lightly. When the fudge has cooled to room temperature, leave it to chill in the fridge for a couple of hours, then remove it from the tin and cut into small squares. Store in an airtight tin.

Apple & blackberry Charlotte

SERVES 6

100g butter
2 tbsp demerara sugar
6 slices of bread, crusts
    removed and halved

FILLING
300g eating apples, peeled
    and diced
squeeze of lemon juice
½ tsp ground cinnamon
35g caster sugar
200g blackberries
a few drops of rosewater
    (optional)

TO SERVE
custard, cream or ice cream

A perfect autumnal delight and there's nothing better than hedgerow hopping to collect your own blackberries. We've always found that a Charlotte is best made with eating apples – Bramleys tend to collapse into a purée – and we like to cook them lightly first for best results.

1. Preheat the oven to 200°C/Fan 180°C/Gas 6. Take a 1-litre pudding basin and grease it liberally with about 25g of the butter, then sprinkle with the demerara sugar. Melt the remaining butter.

2. Flatten the slices of bread – the easiest way is with a rolling pin. Dip the slices in the melted butter, then use most of them to line the pudding basin, making sure they overlap slightly. Reserve a couple of slices to top the pudding later. If there's a gap in the base of the basin, cut a small piece of bread to fill it.

3. To make the filling, put the apples into a saucepan with the lemon juice, cinnamon, sugar and a splash of water. Cover and cook gently until the apples are just tender, then stir in the blackberries. Take the pan off the heat, but leave it covered for a minute or so, to give the blackberries a chance to warm and release some of their juice. Add a few drops of rosewater if you like.

4. Spoon the apples and blackberries into the pudding basin. Top with the reserved bread to create a lid, pressing it down firmly to seal the sides.

5. Place the basin on a baking tray and bake the pudding for 35–40 minutes until the bread is golden brown and crisp. Remove from the oven. Run a palette knife around the edge of the pudding basin to loosen, then turn it out on to a plate.

6. Serve with custard, cream or ice cream.

Chocolate & butterscotch tartlets

Makes 12

PASTRY
125g plain flour, plus extra for dusting
20g cocoa powder
1 tbsp icing sugar
pinch of salt
75g butter, chilled and diced
1 egg yolk
1–2 tbsp ice-cold water or milk

BUTTERSCOTCH FILLING
120g butter
75ml milk
120g light muscovado sugar or light brown soft sugar
25g plain flour
pinch of salt

TOPPING
50g dark chocolate, broken up

These little tarts have a sweet, soft centre – a bit like me and Dave – but the dark chocolate on top and the chocolate pastry balances out the sweetness to perfection.

1. First make the pastry. Put the flour, cocoa and icing sugar into a bowl and add a generous pinch of salt. Add the butter and rub it in until the mixture is the texture of breadcrumbs. Mix in the egg yolk and drizzle in just enough water or milk to form a smooth dough.

2. Roll the dough out on a floured surface and cut out 12 rounds, each 7.5cm in diameter. The finished tartlets look better if you use a crinkled cutter, rather than a straight one. Use the rounds to line the holes of a fairy cake tin. Line each pastry case with a piece of baking parchment and fill with baking beans. Chill for half an hour.

3. Preheat the oven to 180°C/Fan 160°C/Gas 4. Bake the pastry cases for 15 minutes, then remove the parchment and beans and bake for a further 5 minutes or until the pastry is crisp. Remove the pastry from the oven and leave to cool.

4. To make the filling, put the butter into a saucepan with half the milk. Heat until the butter has melted, then bring to the boil. Right away, turn down the heat and stir in the sugar. Stir until the sugar has dissolved and continue to cook for another couple of minutes.

5. Put the flour in a bowl and whisk in the remaining milk to make a fairly thick paste. Drizzle this paste into the pan with butter and sugar mix, whisking constantly as you go. Add a generous pinch of salt. Continue to cook, still whisking constantly, for several minutes until the mixture has thickened a little but is still pourable.

6. Remove the pan from the heat, then strain the mixture through a sieve into a bowl. Leave to cool for at least 5 minutes, then whisk again to make sure it is completely smooth. Spoon scant tablespoons of the butterscotch filling into the pastry cases.

7. Melt the chocolate in a heatproof bowl over a pan of simmering water. Drizzle thin lines of chocolate over the butterscotch. Put the tarts in the fridge and leave them to chill for several hours before eating.

Rhubarb, rosewater & cardamom kulfi

MAKES 4–6

400g rhubarb, cut into chunks
150g caster sugar
300ml evaporated milk
8 cardamom pods, lightly
    crushed
1–2 tbsp rosewater
pinch of salt
100ml kefir
250ml double or whipping
    cream

TO SERVE (OPTIONAL)
dried rose petals
chopped pistachios

We discovered kulfi – the Indian version of ice cream – on our first trip to India and it has become one of my all-time favourite desserts. I love this version with rhubarb and rosewater, but take care when adding the rosewater. Different brands can vary in strength so start gently and keep tasting. You may find you need more or less sugar depending on the sweetness of the rhubarb. If it doesn't taste sweet enough, add another 25 grams of sugar.

1. Preheat the oven to 200°C/Fan 180°C/Gas 6. Put the rhubarb in a roasting tin, sprinkle over 2 tablespoons of the caster sugar, then toss well so the rhubarb is completely coated. Cover the tin with foil and place in the oven for 15 minutes. Take off the foil and roast the rhubarb for a further 10 minutes, then remove from the oven and leave to cool.

2. Put the remaining sugar in a saucepan with the evaporated milk, the cardamom pods, a tablespoon of the rosewater and a pinch of salt. Heat gently, stirring constantly until the sugar has dissolved, then bring just up to boiling point and remove from the heat. Leave to cool for a few minutes, then stir in the kefir. Leave to cool to room temperature.

3. Strain the milk mixture and put it in a blender with the rhubarb. Blitz until smooth, then push the mixture through a sieve to make it extra smooth if you think it is necessary. Chill thoroughly.

4. If you have an ice cream maker, whip the double or whipping cream to the soft, billowy stage, then fold it through the chilled rhubarb mix. Taste and add more rosewater if you like. Churn the mixture in the ice cream maker, then pour it into kulfi moulds, or use small paper cups or tall ramekins. Freeze until solid.

5. If you don't have an ice cream maker, pour the mixture into moulds as above, then every half an hour, whisk with a fork until the mixture is too stiff to stir. Freeze until solid.

6. To serve, remove the kulfis from the freezer and leave them to stand for 10 minutes. Turn them out and sprinkle with a few dried rose petals and/or chopped pistachios if you like.

on one
side or
the other

66 *Dave and I used to love going out for dinner but inevitably, as we pored over the menu, we were troubled by indecision and the desire to try all the tempting things on offer. The result was that we would always order a few side dishes and other extras 'for the table', which everyone knows is just an excuse for over-ordering. The 'table' became an imaginary friend – a friend who ate more than we did!* 99

Griddled cabbage with cashew & chilli paste

SERVES 4

1 cabbage
1 tbsp olive oil
a few Thai basil or coriander
    leaves, finely chopped, to
    garnish
lime wedges, to serve

CASHEW & CHILLI PASTE
1 tbsp olive or vegetable oil
3 shallots, very finely chopped
3 garlic cloves, finely chopped
35g cashew nuts (see method)
1 tbsp sesame seeds
2 tsp chilli powder
2 tsp light brown soft sugar or
    palm sugar
1 tbsp tamarind paste
zest and juice of ½ lime
1 tbsp dark soy or fish sauce
1 tsp sesame oil

Griddling cabbage really brings out the flavour. The paste recipe does make more than you need but don't worry, as it will keep in the fridge for a couple of weeks or can be frozen for use another time.

1. First make the paste. Heat the oil in a small frying pan and add the shallots. Fry them over a medium heat, until the shallot is translucent and browning in places – you want a bit of caramelisation. Add the garlic and cook for another minute or so, then remove from the heat.

2. Put the cashew nuts in a small food processor and chop finely. Add the shallot and garlic mix and all the remaining ingredients except the sesame oil, then pulse to form a thick paste that still has a bit of texture. Transfer 2 tablespoons of the mixture to a bowl and add the teaspoon of sesame oil and enough water to turn it into a brushable paste. Store the rest of the mixture to use another time.

3. Cut the cabbage into about 8 wedges, making sure that each wedge has a little bit of the core so it doesn't fall apart into separate leaves.

4. Heat a large griddle or a frying pan. Rub or drizzle the oil over the cabbage wedges, then griddle or fry them for 3–4 minutes on each side. Keep the heat medium so the pieces of cabbage don't char too much before the cores are tender. You could cover the pan with a cloche or lid to help the cooking along if you like.

5. Brush a little of the paste over the upward-facing cut sides of the cabbage wedges. Flip them over and turn off the heat. Brush the other side and flip them again. Leave them to cook in the residual heat for a couple of minutes. Garnish with a sprinkling of Thai basil or coriander and serve with lime wedges.

Buttered cabbage with nigella seeds

SERVES 4

1 tbsp olive oil
1 small onion, finely chopped
1 tsp nigella seeds
1 green pointed/hispi cabbage, shredded
25g butter
salt and black pepper

This cabbage dish is super-quick to make and goes down a treat with the aubergine and black bean burgers on page 182.

1. Heat the olive oil in a lidded sauté pan. Add the onion and fry it over a medium-high heat until it's translucent and lightly browned.

2. Add the nigella seeds and cabbage, then season with salt and pepper. Continue to fry until the cabbage starts to collapse down, then add a splash of water and cover the pan.

3. Cook for 3–4 minutes until the cabbage has softened, then add the butter. Toss until the butter has melted and the cabbage is glossy, then check the seasoning and serve.

Parmesan-crusted carrots & parsnips

SERVES 4

500g carrots, trimmed,
    peeling optional
500g parsnips
2 tbsp olive oil
leaves from a large rosemary
    sprig, bruised
50g Parmesan, finely grated
salt and black pepper

Nice as a side dish with the brisket on page 208 or with any roast. Use just carrots or parsnips if you prefer or slim wedges of peeled celeriac.

1. Preheat the oven to 200°C/Fan 180°C/Gas 6. Cut the carrots in half lengthways if they are slender or into batons if they are thicker. Cut the parsnips into batons similar in size to the carrots.

2. Bring a pan of water to the boil. Add a generous amount of salt, then the carrots and parsnips. Par-boil the carrots and parsnips for 3 minutes, then drain them thoroughly in a colander and leave them to steam dry for several minutes.

3. Heat the olive oil in a large roasting tin. Add the carrots, parsnips and rosemary leaves, then season with salt and pepper and bake for about 30 minutes, until tender. Sprinkle with the Parmesan and put the tin back in the oven for another 5 minutes.

Roast sweet potatoes with lime garlic butter

SERVES 4

1kg sweet potatoes, diced
1 tbsp olive oil
1 tsp dried oregano
50g butter
zest of 1 lime
1 tsp honey
3 garlic cloves, crushed
salt and black pepper

TO SERVE
2 tbsp finely chopped parsley
   or coriander
generous pinch chilli flakes
   (optional)

A lovely alternative to regular roast potatoes.

1. Preheat the oven to 200°C/Fan 180°C/Gas 6. Put the sweet potatoes into a large roasting tin and drizzle them with oil. Sprinkle over the oregano, then season with plenty of salt and pepper. Roast for about 20 minutes.

2. Melt the butter and whisk in the lime zest, honey and garlic. Pour most of this over the sweet potatoes, reserving a couple of tablespoons. Mix to coat the sweet potatoes, being careful not to tear them if they are stuck to the roasting tin – a palette knife will help with this.

3. Roast the sweet potatoes for another 15–20 minutes until they are tender with crisp edges. Brush with the reserved butter, then sprinkle with parsley or coriander and chilli flakes, if using.

Hash browns

MAKES 8–12

400g floury potatoes, such as
King Edwards, unpeeled
1 medium onion, very finely
chopped
½ tsp dried thyme
½ tsp dried oregano
2 tbsp plain flour
1 egg, beaten
2–3 tbsp olive oil
20–30g butter
salt and black pepper

These are just the job with eggs for brunch or with the bacon chop schnitzels on page 164.

1. Coarsely grate the potatoes on to a tea towel. Bring the sides of the tea towel up to enclose the potato and twist it into a Dick Whittington-style bundle. Squeeze the bundle to get rid of as much of the water in the potatoes as possible.

2. Unwrap the bundle and transfer the grated potatoes to a colander. Add the onion and sprinkle with a teaspoon of salt. Leave to stand for 10 minutes while more liquid is drawn out, then squeeze again.

3. Tip the potatoes into a bowl and season with more salt, plenty of black pepper and the herbs. Add the flour and stir to thoroughly coat the potato, then stir in the egg.

4. Heat a tablespoon of the olive oil in a large frying pan. Add large dollops of the hash brown mix. Leave for several minutes until a rich, golden crust forms underneath, then flip. Add 10g of the butter – it will melt and foam around the hash browns. Continue to cook until the underside has also developed a golden crust.

5. Remove the hash browns from the pan and drain on kitchen paper. Repeat until you have used up all the mixture. Serve hot.

Home fries

SERVES 4

1kg waxy/salad potatoes,
  unpeeled and left whole
1 tbsp cider vinegar
3 tbsp olive oil or 1 tbsp olive
  oil and 2 tbsp dripping
1 large onion, finely chopped
1 garlic clove, finely chopped
1 tsp sweet paprika
1 tsp dried thyme
salt and black pepper

Home fries can be cooked on the hob, but we like this oven-cooked version. Adding vinegar helps the potatoes tenderise without collapsing.

1. Put the potatoes into a large pan and cover with water. Add plenty of salt and the cider vinegar. Bring to the boil and cook for about 10 minutes until the potatoes are just tender. Drain and leave them to cool for a few minutes, then cut them into wedges.

2. Preheat the oven to 200°C/Fan 180°C/Gas 6. Put a roasting tin on the hob and heat for a minute, then add 2 tablespoons of the oil or the dripping. When the fat is really hot, add the potatoes, then put the tin in the oven and roast the potatoes for about 30 minutes.

3. When the potatoes are nearly ready, fry the onion. Heat the remaining tablespoon of olive oil in a frying pan. Add the onion and cook over a medium heat until softened and lightly browned. Add the garlic and cook for another couple of minutes.

4. When the potatoes are done, add the onion and garlic to the roasting tin. Sprinkle over the paprika and thyme and season with salt and pepper. Stir together before serving.

Rice & peas

SERVES 4

1 tbsp coconut or vegetable
  oil
1 onion, finely chopped
200g basmati rice, well rinsed
  and drained
200ml coconut milk
400g can of red kidney beans,
  black beans or gungo peas
1 thyme sprig
¼ tsp ground allspice
salt and black pepper

A perfect partner for the blackened fish on page 152.

1. Warm the oil in a large saucepan over a medium heat, then add the onion. Cook gently for a minute or so, then stir in the rice. Pour in the coconut milk and 400ml of water, then add the beans or gungo peas, thyme and allspice. Season with salt and pepper.

2. Bring to the boil, then turn down the heat to a simmer and cover the pan with a lid. Leave to cook for 15–20 minutes until all the liquid has been absorbed. Take the pan off the heat and leave it to stand, covered, for about 5 minutes, before serving.

Béchamel sauce

MAKES ABOUT 1 LITRE

1 litre whole milk
2 bay leaves
a few peppercorns
a slice of onion
75g butter
75g plain flour
100ml white wine
a grating of nutmeg
salt and black pepper

It's always useful to know how to make a good béchamel sauce and you will need this for the lasagne on page 204.

1. Pour the milk into a saucepan and add the bay leaves, peppercorns and onion slice. Heat very gently until close to boiling, then remove the pan from the heat and leave the milk to cool and infuse.

2. Heat the butter in a saucepan. When it has melted, add the flour and stir to form a thick paste or roux. Add the wine and stir until smooth. Strain the milk and add it to the roux a little at a time. Allow it to boil up in between each addition before stirring thoroughly to make sure you have no lumps. You will end up with a smooth, fairly runny sauce. Add a grating of nutmeg and season with salt and pepper.

Mayonnaise

MAKES A GOOD BOWLFUL

2 egg yolks
1 tsp mustard
250ml sunflower or
    groundnut oil
squeeze of lemon juice or a
    few drops of white wine
    vinegar
salt and black pepper

Obviously you can buy mayonnaise, but the home-made version is something else and so good. It's easier to make than you might think.

1. Put the egg yolks in a bowl with the mustard and a little salt. Mix them together until well combined.

2. Start drizzling in the oil, a few drops at a time, whisking constantly. Continue until you have incorporated all the oil and the mixture has thickened nicely.

3. If the mayonnaise seems to be becoming greasy or too thick to work with, add a few drops of warm water and whisk thoroughly before adding any more oil.

4. Taste the mayonnaise, then season to your liking and add lemon juice or white wine vinegar

Flatbreads

MAKES 8

500g strong white bread flour,
 plus extra for dusting
½ tsp fast-acting dried yeast
2 tsp garlic powder (optional)
1 tsp sugar
1 tsp salt
150ml yoghurt
2 tbsp olive oil
150–200ml tepid water
100g melted butter, for
 basting
mustard, sesame, cumin or
 nigella seeds (optional)

A nice stove-top flatbread. The dough can be made ahead and chilled until you're ready to cook the flatbreads or you can cook them in advance and reheat them over a low heat. Brush with the butter after reheating, not before.

1. Put the flour in a bowl with the yeast, garlic powder, if using, and the sugar. Stir to combine, then stir in the salt. Mix the yoghurt and olive oil together and work them into the dry ingredients. Add enough of the water to make a fairly sticky dough.

2. Turn the dough out on to a floured surface and knead it until smooth. Cover the dough with a damp tea towel and leave it to prove for about an hour until it has increased in size by about a third. If you want to prepare the dough ahead, transfer it to the fridge at this stage.

3. When you're ready to cook, divide the dough into 8 pieces. Roll each one as thinly as you can – aim for a diameter of at least 20–25cm.

4. Heat a dry frying pan. Cook the flatbreads one at a time for 2–3 minutes on each side until cooked through and dappled brown.

5. Brush the flatbreads generously with the butter, and sprinkle with your choice of seeds, if using.

Tahdig – crispy Persian rice

SERVES ABOUT 8

400g basmati rice
a large pinch of saffron
75g Greek yoghurt
100g butter, melted
2 tbsp olive oil
sea salt

Rice with a beautifully crispy crust on the base. Delicious.

1. Put the rice in a bowl and cover it with water. Swirl around until the water is cloudy, then strain. Repeat several times until the water is virtually clear. Cover the rice with fresh water and leave it to stand for half an hour.

2. Fill a large pan with plenty of freshly boiled water. Add a heaped teaspoon of salt and bring it back to the boil, then add the rice and boil for about 5 minutes until partially cooked. Drain the rice and rinse under cold water.

3. Meanwhile, use a pestle and mortar to crush the saffron with a generous pinch of sea salt. Add 2 tablespoons of freshly boiled water and leave to steep for 10 minutes.

4. Put the yoghurt in a bowl and drizzle over a tablespoon of the saffron water. Add 300g of the parboiled rice and mix thoroughly. Stir in a couple of tablespoons of the melted butter.

5. Heat the oil in a shallow flameproof casserole dish with a lid – about 25-28cm in diameter is ideal. Add the rice mixture, spreading it as evenly as you can and pressing it down lightly. Mix a teaspoon of salt with the remaining rice and sprinkle it over the top. Using the handle of a wooden spoon, poke holes into the rice – this will help steam escape from the bottom of the pan and help the crisping up of the bottom layer. Mix the remaining saffron water with the rest of the melted butter. Pour this over the top of the rice, allowing some to drip into the holes.

6. Wrap the lid of the pan or dish in a tea towel and place it on top. Cook over a medium heat for about 10 minutes, then turn the heat down to very low and leave to cook and allow the crust to form. If you're cooking on gas, don't leave the centre of the pan in the centre of the burner for the entire cooking time – move it around every few minutes. This will ensure that the rice cooks evenly and doesn't burn in the middle.

7. Start checking the crust after about 25 minutes, it can take up to 40. Lift an edge of the rice with a palette knife – if it's starting to look crisp and brown around the edges, it should be done. Remove from the heat and leave to stand – with the tea towel and lid in place – for 5 minutes.

8. To turn out, go round the edges carefully with a palette knife, checking to see if the crust comes away cleanly. When you are sure you have a good chance of it turning out intact, upturn the pan on to a large serving dish. It should come away cleanly. If it doesn't, pull the crust off separately and arrange it over the top – this is a perfectly acceptable way to serve it!

Cornbread

225g fine or coarse cornmeal
½ tsp bicarbonate of soda
½ tsp baking powder
15g caster sugar
½ tsp salt
284ml carton of buttermilk
3 eggs, beaten
50g butter
2 tbsp maple syrup
salt

Cornbread is quick and easy to make – no rising needed. Great with the brisket on page 208.

1. Preheat the oven to 200°C/Fan 180°C/Gas 6. You need either a 20cm skillet or a round ovenproof dish or baking tin.

2. Put the cornmeal, bicarbonate of soda, baking powder, sugar and salt in a bowl. Mix the buttermilk and eggs together and add them to the dry ingredients. Combine, keeping the mixing to an absolute minimum.

3. Melt half the butter directly in your skillet, dish or tin, then pour in the cornbread batter. Bake in the oven for 25–30 minutes until the cornbread is well risen and golden brown.

4. Remove from the oven. Melt the remaining butter and maple syrup together and drizzle the mixture over the cornbread, letting it sizzle down the sides. This is best served hot from the oven, cut into wedges.

Thai curry paste

2 banana shallots

2 lemongrass stalks, soft
   centres only

5g root ginger, roughly
   chopped

10g galangal, roughly
   chopped

6 garlic cloves, roughly
   chopped

4 medium red chillies, roughly
   chopped

2–4 red Thai chillies,
   (according to taste),
   roughly chopped

4 lime leaves, roughly
   chopped

zest and juice of 1 lime

2 tbsp finely chopped
   coriander root or stems

1 tsp ground coriander

1 tsp ground cumin

1 tsp shrimp paste

½ tsp turmeric

1 tsp salt

Use this paste for the Thai pot-roast chicken on page 202.

Use this paste for the Thai pot-roast chicken on page 202.

1. Put everything in a food processor and pulse until well broken down into a paste. Add a splash of water if necessary to help form the paste.

2. Store in a jar in the fridge for up to a week.

Enchilada spice mix

MAKES 3–4 TBSP

1 tbsp dried oregano
1 tbsp ground cumin
2 tsp garlic powder
1 tsp ground cinnamon
1 tsp ground allspice
1 tsp chilli powder

Make this for the chicken enchiladas on page 190.

1. Mix all the ingredients together and store in an airtight jar.

Dhansak curry powder

MAKES ABOUT 5 TBSP

1 tbsp coriander seeds
1 tbsp cumin seeds
1 tbsp crushed chilli flakes or
    dried chillies
1 tsp green cardamom pods
1 tsp black peppercorns
1 tsp fenugreek seeds
1 tsp mustard seeds
6 cloves
2 black cardamom pods
1 star anise or 1 tsp aniseed
3cm cinnamon stick
¼ tsp ground nutmeg
1 tsp ground turmeric

Perfect for the chicken dhansak on page 194.

1. First, toast all the whole spices in a frying pan, shaking the pan regularly until they give off an intense aroma. Transfer them to a plate to cool.

2. Grind the whole spices in a spice grinder, then add the nutmeg and turmeric. Store in an airtight jar.

Sauté potatoes

SERVES 4

800g potatoes, preferably
    Maris Pipers
50g butter
1 tbsp olive oil
1 small bulb of garlic, cloves
    separated but unpeeled
1 tsp finely chopped fresh
    thyme leaves
salt and black pepper

These beautifully crunchy potatoes are great served with the duck à l'orange on page 192 or with almost anything for that matter.

1. Cut the potatoes into chunks of about 2.5cm. Put them in a pan, add water to cover, then bring them to the boil. Reduce the heat slightly and leave the potatoes to simmer for 5 minutes.

2. Drain the potatoes and leave them in the colander to dry for a few minutes. Then shake the colander from side to side to bash the edges of the potatoes a little – this will give nice crispy edges.

3. Melt the butter in a large non-stick frying pan and add the oil. Add the potatoes and season them with salt and lots of pepper. Fry over a medium-low heat for 10 minutes, stirring occasionally.

4. Scatter the garlic cloves into the pan and continue to cook for about 15 minutes, turning regularly, until the potatoes are golden brown and the garlic has softened. Sprinkle in the thyme leaves and cook for another 5 minutes, stirring and turning the potatoes.

Chinese pancakes

MAKES 20

225g plain flour
salt
2 tsp sesame oil, plus more
    for frying

You can. of course. buy the pancakes for the Chinese duck recipe on page 198. but it's very satisfying to make your own.

1. Put the flour in a bowl with a generous pinch of salt. Pour over 150ml of water which has been boiled and left to stand for 5 minutes – it should be around 80°C – then drizzle in the 2 teaspoons of oil. Mix together and as soon as the mixture is cool enough to handle, knead for several minutes until you have a smooth dough.

2. Divide the dough into 20 pieces. These will look smaller than you expect, but they will roll out very thinly and stretch. Roll each one as flat and as round as you can get it – aim for a diameter of about 16cm.

3. To cook the pancakes, heat a frying pan and rub it with a few drops of sesame oil. Fry each pancake over a medium heat until cooked on the underside and lightly speckled with brown spots. Flip and cook the top side – they should immediately puff up but will deflate as they cool. Keep warm if using immediately. Alternatively, wrap the pancakes in foil and reheat by steaming for several minutes.

Chicken & pork ramen stock

MAKES AT LEAST 3 LITRES

1.5kg raw chicken carcasses,
  pulled apart
1.5kg pork bones, preferably
  spare ribs
1 pig's trotter
1 onion, skin included if clean
  enough, roughly chopped
2 carrots, roughly chopped
30g root ginger, roughly
  chopped
1 head of garlic, cloves
  separated but unpeeled

This is a perfect stock for the ramen on page 82. it's enough to make two quantities of ramen and it freezes well. but if you don't want to make so much, just half the quantities.

1. Put the carcasses, pork bones and the pig's trotter in a large stock pot that holds 8–10 litres of water. Cover them with cold water and bring to the boil. When a mushroom-coloured foam starts to appear, start skimming it off. Continue skimming until the foam that appears is white.

2. Meanwhile, heat a griddle pan over a high heat. When it's too hot to hold your hand over – don't touch the pan – add the onion, carrots and ginger. Griddle the vegetables for several minutes, turning regularly, until fairly dark char lines appear on them.

3. Reduce the heat under the stock pot slightly so the broth is bubbling, not fiercely but harder than a simmer. Add the onion, carrots, ginger and garlic, then partially cover the pan and cook the broth for at least 3 hours or up to 5 if you can. Keep an eye on the liquid level. The stock shouldn't reduce too much, but don't let it boil away in the first hour or so and top it up with more water if necessary.

4. When the broth is a deep golden-brown and quite cloudy, strain it through a sieve. As this is such a rich stock, it is a good idea to skim off some of the fat. Do this when the fat settles on top or chill the broth until the fat has set and just scrape it off.

Vegetable stock

MAKES ABOUT 1.5 LITRES

1 tsp olive oil
2 large onions, roughly
    chopped
3 large carrots, chopped
200g squash or pumpkin,
    unpeeled, diced
4 celery sticks, sliced
2 leeks, sliced
100ml white wine or
    vermouth
large thyme sprig
large parsley sprig
1 bay leaf
a few black peppercorns

1. Heat the olive oil in a large saucepan. Add all the vegetables and fry them over a high heat, stirring regularly, until they start to brown and caramelise around the edges. This will take at least 10 minutes. Add the white wine or vermouth and boil until it has evaporated away.

2. Cover the vegetables with 2 litres of water, add the herbs and black peppercorns and bring to the boil. Turn the heat down to a gentle simmer, then continue to cook the stock, uncovered, for about an hour, stirring now and then.

3. Strain the stock through a colander lined with muslin or kitchen paper into a bowl. Store it in the fridge for up to a week or freeze it.

Fish stock

MAKES ABOUT 1.5 LITRES

1.5kg fish heads and bones
    from white fish (ask your
    fishmonger)
1 tbsp salt
2 tbsp olive oil
1 onion, finely chopped
2 leeks, finely sliced
½ fennel bulb, finely chopped
1 celery stick, sliced
2 garlic cloves, sliced
200ml white wine
bouquet garni, made up of
    2 sprigs each of parsley,
    tarragon and thyme
2 bay leaves
a few black peppercorns
1 piece of thinly pared lemon
    zest

1. Put the fish heads and bones in a bowl, cover them with cold water and add the salt. Leave to stand for an hour, then drain them and wash thoroughly under running water. This process helps to draw out any blood from the fish and gives you a much clearer, fresher-tasting stock.

2. Heat the olive oil in a large saucepan. Add the onion, leeks, fennel, celery and garlic. Cook the vegetables over a medium heat for several minutes until they start to soften without taking on any colour.

3. Add the fish heads and bones and pour over the wine. Bring to the boil, then add 2 litres of water. Bring back to the boil, skim off any mushroom-coloured foam that appears on the surface, then turn the heat down to a very slow simmer. Add the herbs, peppercorns and lemon zest and leave to simmer for 30 minutes, skimming off any foam every so often.

4. Strain the stock through a colander or sieve into a bowl, then line the sieve with muslin or kitchen paper and strain the stock again. Don't try to push it through as that will result in a cloudier stock. Leave to cool, then store it in the fridge for up to 3 or 4 days or freeze it.

Chicken stock

MAKES ABOUT 1 LITRE

at least 1 chicken carcass, pulled apart
4 chicken wings (optional)
1 onion, unpeeled, cut into quarters
1 large carrot, cut into large chunks
2 celery sticks, roughly chopped
1 leek, roughly chopped
1 tsp black peppercorns
3 bay leaves
large parsley sprig
small thyme sprig
a few garlic cloves, unpeeled (optional)

1. Put the chicken bones and the wings, if using, into a saucepan that's just large enough for all the chicken to fit quite snugly. Cover with cold water, bring to the boil, then skim off any foam that collects. Add the remaining ingredients and turn the heat down to a very low simmer. Partially cover the pan with a lid.

2. Leave the stock to simmer for about 3 hours, then remove the pan from the heat. Strain the stock through a colander lined with muslin or kitchen paper into a bowl.

3. The stock can be used right away, although it is best to skim off most of the fat that will collect on the top. If you don't need the stock immediately, leave it to cool. The fat will set on top and will be much easier to remove.

4. You can keep the stock in the fridge for up to 5 days or freeze it. If you want to make a larger amount of stock, save up your chicken carcasses in the freezer or add more chicken wings.

Beef stock

MAKES ABOUT 2 LITRES

1.5kg beef bones, including marrow bones if possible, cut into small lengths
500g piece of beef shin or any cheap, fairly lean cut
2 onions, unpeeled, roughly chopped
1 leek, roughly chopped
2 celery sticks, roughly chopped
2 carrots, roughly chopped
2 tomatoes
½ tsp peppercorns
bouquet garni, made up of large sprigs of thyme, parsley and 2 bay leaves

1. Put the beef bones and meat into a large saucepan and cover them with cold water – you'll need at least 3–3.5 litres. Bring the water to the boil and when a starchy, mushroom-grey foam appears, start skimming. Keep on skimming as the foam turns white and continue until it has almost stopped developing.

2. Add the vegetables, peppercorns and bouquet garni. Turn down the heat until the stock is simmering very gently, then partially cover the pan with a lid. Leave to simmer for 3–4 hours.

3. Line a colander with 2 layers of muslin or kitchen paper and place it over a large bowl. Ladle the stock into the sieve or colander to strain it. Remove the meat and set it aside, then discard everything else. Pour the strained stock into a large container and leave it to cool. The fat should solidify on top of the stock and will be very easy to remove. You can keep the stock in the fridge for 2 or 3 days or freeze it.

4. Don't chuck out the piece of meat – it's good in sandwiches or can be sliced, fried and added to salads.

Lemon curd

MAKES 750G

4 eggs
4 egg yolks
250g caster sugar
200ml lemon juice
zest of 3 lemons
150g unsalted butter, cut into
    small cubes

Make this for the lemon curd and hazelnut slices on page 226 or just to slather on your morning toast.

1. Whisk the eggs and egg yolks in a large heatproof bowl until well combined. Add the sugar and stir in the lemon juice and zest. Add the butter, then set the bowl over a saucepan of very gently simmering water, making sure the bottom of the bowl doesn't touch the water.

2. Stir the mixture with a wooden spoon for 5 minutes until the butter melts, then cook for 10–12 minutes, whisking constantly. The lemon curd should have the consistency of custard and the whisk should leave a light trail when lifted. The curd will continue to thicken as it cools.

3. Pour the hot lemon curd into warm, sterilised jars and leave to cool. Cover the surface of the curd with a disc of waxed paper or baking parchment and seal with a lid. Keep the curd in the fridge and use within a couple of weeks.

TIP

To sterilise jars, put them through a hot dishwasher cycle or wash them in hot, soapy water, rinse thoroughly and dry them in a low oven. Make sure the jars are completely dry before filling.

Coconut ice cream

MAKES 750G

50g desiccated or shredded
   coconut
4 egg yolks
125g caster sugar
1 tbsp cornflour
pinch of salt
400ml coconut milk
300ml double cream

If you're into making your own ice cream, try this for the baked Alaska on page 232.

1. First toast the desiccated or shredded coconut. Put it in a dry frying pan and toast, stirring regularly, until lightly browned. Do not leave the coconut unattended, as it can catch very quickly. Tip it into a bowl and leave to cool.

2. In another bowl, whisk the egg yolks with the sugar, cornflour and a pinch of salt until pale and well aerated. The mixture will be quite stiff to work with initially but will loosen up as air is incorporated. Pour in the coconut milk and whisk to combine, then tip it all into a saucepan.

3. Stir over a low-medium heat until the mixture thickens into a custard. Remove from the heat and pour the mixture into a fridge-proof container. Leave to cool, then chill in the fridge for at least an hour. Whisk in the double cream and stir in the toasted coconut.

4. Churn the ice cream until thick if you have an ice cream maker. Alternatively, put the mixture in the freezer and whisk thoroughly every half an hour until it is too stiff to work.

5. Freeze for several hours or overnight, then remove from the freezer about 15 minutes before you want to serve it.

Index

S

MY HEARTFELT THANKS

I want to take this opportunity to express my love and thanks to all the people mentioned below for their kindness, endless support and cuddles, as well as for the laughter and tears we've had together while completing this book after Dave's passing. I would also like to thank Lil, Dave's devoted wife, for her support and encouragement with the book. Lil brought Dave so much happiness during the years they had together.

Massive thanks to Catherine Phipps, Andrew Hayes-Watkins, Lucie Stericker, Jinny Johnson, Hattie Baker, Rachel Vere and Stevie Taylor for all your help with the recipes, text and photographs, and to Elise See Tai for proofreading and Vicki Robinson for indexing.

Many thanks also Vicky Eribo, Anna Valentine, Jess Hart, Virginia Woolstencroft, Francesca Pearce, Tom Noble, Louis Patel, Jennifer Wilson, Catherine Worsley, Victoria Laws, Esther Waters, Lucy Horrocks, Natalie Dawkins, Helen Ewing and Tierney Witty at The Orion Publishing Group for all their support.

And as always huge love and thanks to Nicola Ibison, Tasha Hall, Roland Carreras, Barrie Simpson and Francesca Sheppard at the Ibison Talent Group, and to Nicole Kavanagh, my amazing PA.

Love you all so much,

Si xxx

Dedication

To Dave, I love you and I miss you.

First published in Great Britain in 2024 by Seven Dials,
an imprint of The Orion Publishing Group Ltd
Carmelite House, 50 Victoria Embankment
London EC4Y 0DZ

An Hachette UK Company

10 9 8 7 6 5 4 3 2 1

A CIP catalogue record for this book is available from the British Library.

ISBN (Hardback): 978 1 3996 0732 2
ISBN (eBook): 978 1 3996 0733 9

Publisher: Vicky Eribo
Editor: Jinny Johnson
Recipe consultant: Catherine Phipps
Photography: Andrew Hayes-Watkins
Design & art direction: Lucie Stericker, Studio 7:15
Food stylist: Hattie Baker
Food stylist's assistant: Stevie Taylor
Props stylist: Rachel Vere
Senior production controller: Lucy Horrocks
Cover design: Jessica Hart

Origination by F1 Colour Ltd., London
Printed in Germany

www.orionbooks.co.uk